The
MIRROR
Challenge

Petal L. Miller

'The power of The MIRROR Challenge
lies in its simplicity'

The
MIRЯOR
Challenge

Petal L. Miller

PLM Publishing

PLM Publishing
Email: info@themirrorchallenge.com
www.themirrorchallenge.com

ISBN 978 – 1 – 5272 – 6275 - 1

Dedication

This book is dedicated to my parents, the late Alva and Sarah Miller; who taught me to be me - who I am, gave me my identity and values; such as a passion for reading, writing and learning, a quest for knowledge and most of all, an inquisitive mind. I believe that curiosity is the key to life. They showed me how to approach the world and life. They were simply the best parents and teachers, a girl could ever have wanted. Their souls are now at peace.

I am also dedicating this book to my two brilliant, wonderful, loving and marvellous sisters, Kesey and Zona Miller. It has been great growing up with you guys. I would not have wanted life any other way. We have always been there for each other. You have been my rock and mirrors and I have learnt so much from you.

Acknowledgements

There are so many people that I would like to thank for their tremendous help, suggestions, thoughts, ideas and words of encouragement regarding this book, especially the participants – the managers, staff and the various groups that I have trained and worked with over the many years. You have been my treasure troves, my ocean of wisdom and my fountain of knowledge. I have learnt so much from you and you have definitely made a difference in my life and other people's lives. Thank you for your brilliant insights, feedback and time and allowing me to have you as 'mirrors' – gilt edged mirrors. What a reflection and revelation it has been! You have really lifted me and given me the impetus and the drive to finish this book.

This book has been a true labour of love. In particular, I would like to thank Richard Larmond and Elaine Carr for their wonderful help, advice and support during the writing and revision process of this book. Thank you both for inspiring and motivating me to complete this update. Without you pushing me every step of the way, I don't think I would have gotten this far. What an extraordinary and awesome journey it has been; at times looking and feeling insurmountable. However we knew we could see the invisible and do the impossible. To God, be the glory for the great and wonderful things He is doing in our lives!

Contents

Contents

About the Author

Petal L. Miller is an experienced Human Resource professional with an extensive portfolio in the People Management and Development field. Her client base is varied, encompassing the public, private and voluntary sectors, nationally and internationally. She holds a Master's degree in Human Resource Management, specialising in Human Resource Development. She is a Chartered member of the Chartered Institute of Personnel and Development (CIPD). She has been involved in education, learning, training and development since 1977. Petal is passionate about children and people and believes that her role in life is to facilitate the growth and development of others.

In 1997, she established **PLM Development Services**. Petal inspires, motivates and guides individuals to think and operate 'outside of the box' and to make positive changes to their lives, whether it is helping people to build new careers or to simply add skills to their existing portfolio. She is an enabler of learning rather than a presenter of information and facts. Her training programmes are heavily based on personal self-development. Her primary objective is to ensure that there is a 'holistic approach' to people development, performance and career management.

Petal is the Trainer's Trainer. She specialises in designing and facilitating innovative management and leadership development programmes and strategies which enable individuals, teams and organisations to meet their goals and facilitate personal and professional growth and development. As well as being a creative and results oriented executive coach, she is also an extremely energetic conference facilitator and a highly experienced presentation and skills trainer. Petal is the specialist in re-igniting passion in businesses and individuals. She is a 'people person,' who touches your heart as well as your soul. She makes you laugh, but importantly, she makes you think! According to a delegate – 'Petal has given my brain a workout!'

She is a dynamic speaker who gets her ideas and the message across with clarity and passion. An intriguing combination of humour and ability makes Petal an outstanding presenter. She has become well known for her sound practical approach to training. Petal regularly receives high praises from participants for her refreshing, thought-provoking and informative delivery. You will appreciate her innovative and participatory techniques that produce immediate gains in your personal productivity and learning.

She is the founder of **Women Celebrating Women**, a networking forum for women to encourage, elevate, educate, empower and celebrate each other. The forum provides the platform for women to share their learning and expertise, strengthen each other through their experiences and challenges, capitalise on career and business opportunities, build unbelievable personal connections, be in the company of great women - their energy and dynamism - and most importantly, celebrate and recognise each other's uniqueness, differences as well as achievements!

What others are saying about this book . . .

Dear Pastor Petal, we had a brilliant class last night sharing from your book, "The Mirror Challenge". Some of the comments from the students included: "Very engaging session", "Thought provoking", "reflective", "challenging" us to strive for GOLD!

From one of the Pastors: "Bishop it was nice for every participant to look his or herself in the mirror and define who he/she is. Self-appraisal is key to personal development both socially and spiritually. Petal has always been a good public educator and coach. She has done some work for us in the past in my Department."

Bishop Ian Patterson-Sharpe, March 2020

Petal is touching people's lives – that's what you do best! Total job satisfaction!

Elizabeth Uwadiae, October 2018

I thank you so much for taking the time out to write: "The Mirror Challenge". This book has been really encouraging and has made me look at things differently.

"What others think or say about me is none of my business. Knowing who I am is more important." I would definitely recommend this insightful book, which I believe could be life changing to many. Thank you Petal L. Miller, you're truly an amazing and inspirational woman.

#onwardandupwards

Yasmin Thompson, January 2019

Petal, as the dynamic trainer and teacher that she is, has taken her wealth of knowledge and wisdom and crafted it into a fantastic book that caters for all learning preferences. The book is packed with information, tools, questions and exercises. The Mirror Challenge is a must-read for you if you want to understand yourself better and will inspire you to challenge yourself. If you are thinking of how to take your career and life to the next level or break free from living a life of mediocrity and unfulfilled dreams, this is a book for you.

The book will teach you how to break free from doubt and achieve your full potential. In this book, Petal shares powerful principles; that if applied will transform your life to greater heights. It is a practical book, written in a simple, easy to read style for all ages. It shows how anyone can aim high, move fast and excel. Don't just read the book, but implement the ideas in this book. That is where the true power of this book resides. So, take immediate action on the ideas in the book and it will change the course and direction of your life. I highly recommend this book.

Dayo Olomu, April 2019

Amazing read, I recommend this book to everyone. So many useful hints and tips and a real eye opener about how you could be doing things differently.

Amy Shepherd, April 2019

'Don't ask for permission, ask for forgiveness'

★ ★ ★ ★ ★ This book is amazing, I love its distinctive features and humour; at the same time drawing narratives on everyday skills, strengths, values and self-worth.

Sheva Waite, June 2019

The Mirror Challenge by Petal L Miller is an excellent, practical and easy to read workbook which you can implement in your daily life. It is good for all age groups at different stages in their lives and applicable to everyone who needs it.

Whenever I pick up the book and open its pages, I feel inspired, empowered and challenged to improve my life in different areas. This book comes highly recommended and you will not be disappointed.

Dr. Joan Myers OBE, QN, RN June 2019

Introduction

In 1999, a colleague sent me an email which contained the following words:

'Everything is much further away now than it used to be. It is twice as far to the corner, and they added a hill, I have noticed.

I have given up running for the bus, it leaves so much faster than it used to. It seems to me that they are making steps steeper than in the old days. Have you noticed how much smaller the print is that they use in the newspapers now?

There is no use in asking anyone to read aloud to me as everyone speaks in such a low voice that I can hardly hear them. The material in clothes is getting so skimpy, especially around the waist and hips.

Even people are changing; they are so much younger than they used to be when I was their age. On the other hand people of my own age are so much older than I am. I ran into an old friend the other day and she had aged so much that she did not even recognise me.

*I got to thinking about the poor thing while I was combing my hair this morning and in doing so I glanced at my reflection and was confounded – **they don't even make good mirrors like they used to!!'***

At the end of reading this, especially the line, which I think is funny, which states, **'they don't even make good mirrors like they used to'**, it resonated in my spirit for a long time. I am a fan of acronyms and in 2004, I thought about the letters of the word mirror and penned the acronym **MIRROR - M**irror, **I**mpact, **R**eflect, **R**espond, **O**pportunities and **R**esults. This also coincided with the decision to develop a one and two day personal development training programme, **The MIRROR Challenge™**.

Having successfully run this programme over the years within organisations, businesses, and with a variety of groups at conferences, seminars, workshops and other events, I kept on being asked, where is the book? I initially developed **The MIRROR Challenge Workbook** and I have been 'challenged' a number of times to convert the workbook into this book from delegates who have been inspired and positively benefited from engaging in the **MIRROR Challenge** experience.

The dilemma that we all face is to ask ourselves where we are going in terms of our lives. One of my favourite words is 'Next!' What is next for me? For some readers who are in a bit of a rut, you could be wondering what's happening to me and/or why am I here? Have you been watching a 'movie' lately that seems to be stuck on the repeat button? Have you been caught in a maze and can't see your way out? It makes sense, every once in a while to step back from your day to day activities and ask yourself: Who I am? What am I doing? Where am I? Where am I going? Why am I here? How am I doing? What and where do I need to make changes?

The MIRROR Challenge™ is aimed at challenging you to challenge yourself. It is about empowering your future. The book is overflowing with inspiration, innovation and practical solutions that you can implement straightaway. Throughout the book, there are a series of questions for you to think about and find answers. Each chapter of the book consists of a series of questions relating to each letter of the word 'MIRROR' – to get you to provocatively think about all aspects of your life. There are also a number of tried and tested MIRROR Challenge Exercises in each chapter as well as 'Have a Mirror Moment!' Exercise. These are for you to complete on your own initially. When you have finished, find a partner, colleague or friend and share the questions and answers with each other. The true purpose of the questions and the exercises is to help you get a fresh and new insight as well as a different perspective of who you are and 'unearth' the real picture/reflection of you. Be authentic. You need to be honest, truthful and frank with yourself, or you will end up as someone else and that's not who you want to be.

The book is not about weight, height, dress size or body image. It is about you looking in the mirror of life metaphorically and challenging yourself, your reflection, your thoughts, your vision, your mind, your feelings, your senses - what you see, hear, feel. Most importantly, this book is about what action you need to take to change your current situation (if you don't like it) and taking it!

The MIRROR Challenge™ is for everyone – whether you are in work, out of work, between jobs, at a crossroads, at home, semi-retired or retired. It has been written to enable you to:

- Develop a clear understanding of your position, purpose and potential in life

- Have an overview of the skills, tools and techniques needed to enhance your life prospects

- Analyse your **SAKE**

Skills
Abilities
Knowledge and
Experiences

- Examine barriers and obstacles to your self-development and how you overcame or can overcome them

- Identify a range of activities, strategies, routes and opportunities to support you through this journey

- Develop a positive mental attitude towards the pursuance of your tangible and realistic goals

- Identify and set achievable personal steps you need to take to achieve them

- Develop a healthy desire towards achieving success in all areas of your life

This book examines and highlights what makes it possible for people to progress while others struggle to meet their aspirations. The **MIRROR Challenge** is not only a book you read, it's a resource. It has tips and techniques and is a toolkit for you to use. Use it to break new ground and create opportunities in your life. Use it to jump start a stalling career. Use the **MIRROR Challenge** to get to the real you. It is about reading or looking at something again, but with a fresh pair of eyes. It provides practical advice on moving on and getting ahead in life. The **MIRROR Challenge** is a book for inspiring the future. It provides opportunities for individuals to think, plan, do, review and take 'real' action regarding their future. It also aims to assist them in making informed choices and decisions and to take actions to develop themselves proactively.

You may have heard of the bucket or mannequin challenge. Well long before these challenges, was the **MIRROR Challenge**! Are you ready for the **MIRROR Challenge?**

The more you look in the mirror, is the more you will find out about yourself and what changes you need to make to take you to the next level. Remember, the only person who can help you is the person looking back at you in the mirror.

So, here's to looking in the Mirror, taking action and making those life changes.

The MIRROR Challenge - Touching Lives, Transforming Minds!

Mirror

Impact

Reflect

Respond

Opportunities

Results

Give Yourself the MIRROR Challenge!

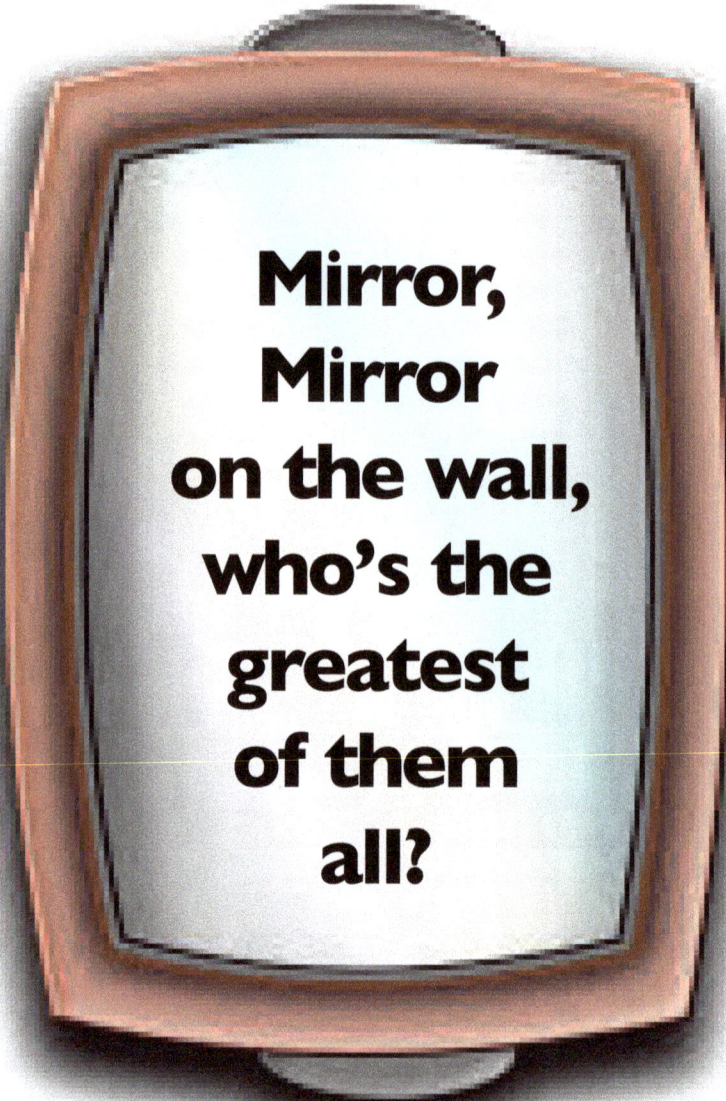

Mirror, Mirror on the wall, who's the greatest of them all?

Chapter One

I Dare You to . . . .

'I Dare You To . . .'
Look in the mirror
and dare yourself!

What is the toughest decision that you will have to make? This is not a trick question. The answer is simple - It is about **YOU**. Everything in your life is a mirror. The aim of the MIRROR Challenge is to ask yourself a series of questions; which requires you to think, reflect and most importantly take positive action about your life and future. As they say, 'Think, Ink, Do and Review'.

MIRROR Challenge Exercise:

Has someone ever dared you?

It could be very realistic or as imaginative as you want the dare to be. You can have more than one dare. It's up to you! Complete the following challenge:

'I Dare You To . . .'

-
-
-
-

Why that particular dare(s)?

How do you plan to achieve your dare(s)?

'Achieving Your Dare(s)'

As the SAS Motto

He Who Dares Wins!

Have a Mirror Moment!

If you are looking for that person to change your life, just look in the MIRROR!

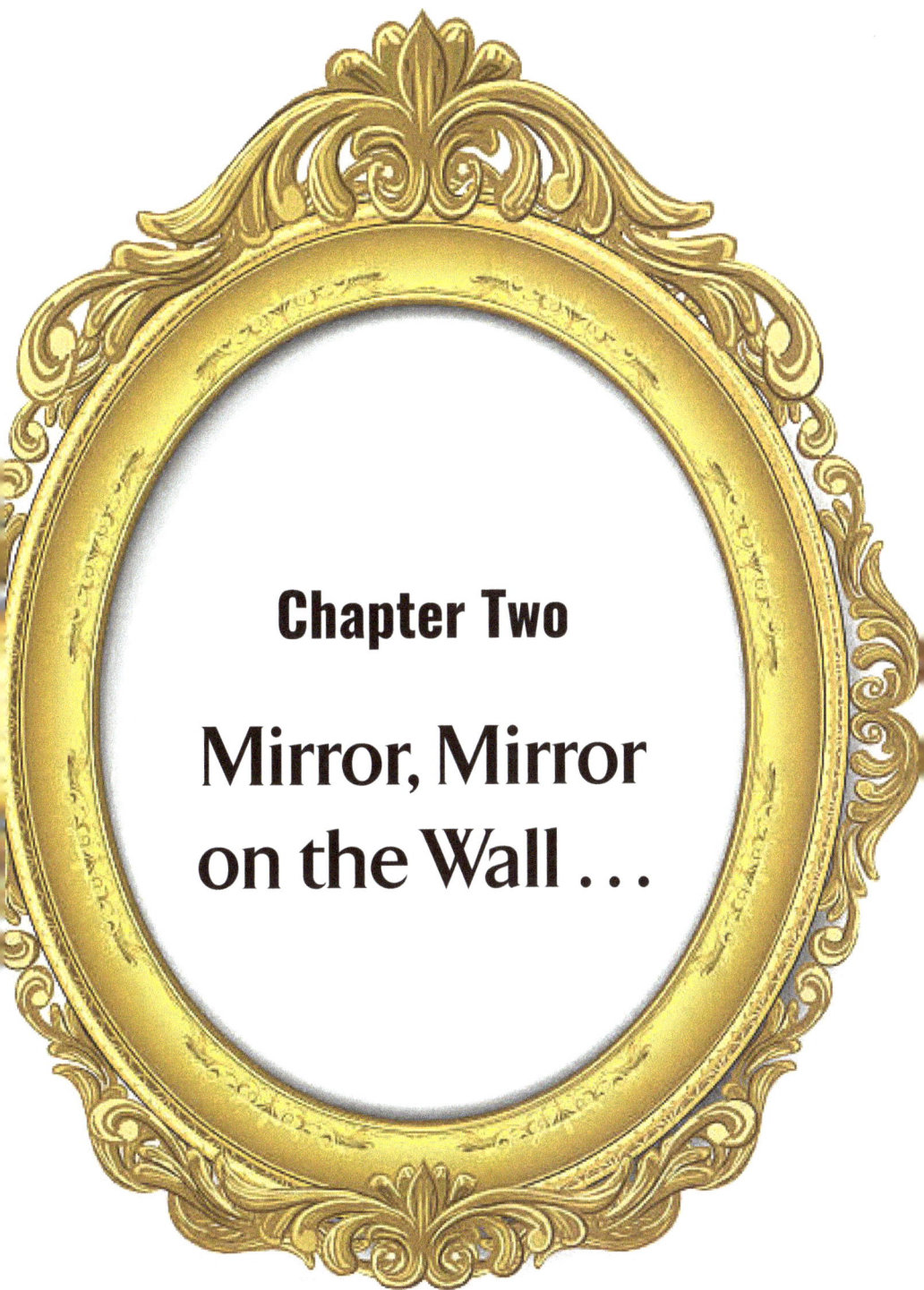

Chapter Two

Mirror, Mirror on the Wall ...

What's the purpose of a mirror?

A mirror has been defined as a surface that is able to reflect light, often used to form an image of an object placed in front of it. This reflecting surface, is usually of glass with a silvery, metallic, or amalgam backing. Interestingly, another definition of a mirror is any reflecting surface, as of calm water under certain lighting conditions. A mirror is something that gives a faithful representation, image, or idea of something else. Most of us are aware of a mirror in terms of furniture, where a reflecting surface is mounted in a frame. Most of the time, we use a mirror to just look at or scrutinise ourselves.

Facing Your MIRROR

Do you own a mirror? Well, it's time to pick it up. What will make you face your mirror? Look at yourself in the mirror and face who you are. What do you see? Who do you see staring back at you? Do you need to apologise to yourself?

'We have to look in the MIRROR whether we want to or not! Whether we admit it or not!'

When looking in the mirror, what do you do?

Do you:
Look?
Glance?
Observe?
Stare?
Look away?

Have you looked in the mirror lately? The Mirror – looking at yourself and deciding what you need to do or change. It's about you competing with yourself and not with others. The only competition is with you!

Looking in the Mirror, Questions to ask yourself:

● Who do you see?

● What do you see?

● Do you see you?

● Who are you? You may know your name, but do you really know who you are?

● What are you?

- Who is the real you?

- What do you see first?

- What is obvious and tangible?

- What do you do?

- What are you capable of doing?

- Where are you going?

- How are you doing?

- How do you define yourself?

- Are you defined by role(s)? Responsibilities?

- What is unique or special about you?

- What are your doubts and fears?

- Do you like what you see?

- Is looking in the mirror hard for you? If Yes, why?

- Do you give value to looking in the mirror?

There is the need to see clearly in the mirror. Is it dusty? Is it clean? Over my years of designing and delivering training programmes, some participants have indicated that they have looked in the mirror but were not looking clearly. One participant actually said, 'It was a lot less me and a lot more of others'.

Others have indicated that looking in the mirror produced fear issues. Have you ever looked in the mirror and thought they don't make good mirrors like they use to? Michael Jackson, once sang *'I'm talking to the man in the mirror. I'm telling him to change his ways'*.

When you move away from the mirror, you forget what you look like. You need to see your reflection in the mirror and take action. Most importantly, ask yourself: "What do I need to change about me and why?" My favourite word is '*how*' - how are you going to make these changes?

Get Ready for Change - The MIRROR wants you to change

For some people including myself, it's not poor or bad decisions that we made but NOT making decisions at all! Procrastination leads to hesitation which does not lead you to your destination!

'Procrastination leads to hesitation and does not lead you to your destination!'

Your SAKE

SKILLS
ABILITIES
KNOWLEDGE
EXPERIENCES

- What skills, abilities, knowledge and experiences do you possess?

- What are Skills?

- What are your Abilities? (How do you undertake your skills?)

- How Knowledgeable are you?

- What are your Experiences?

Life Skills

What are the essential skills that are needed to balance your life and create long and lasting fulfilment?

Identifying Your Skills

Mirror Challenge Skills Exercise:

You Have 5 Minutes To List 20 Skills That You Use In Your Life.

How did you find doing this exercise?

Author's Reflection

Most participants have expressed difficulty in completing the exercise. This had nothing to do with the time, but actually listing their skills. Discussions often follow on: What is a skill? What skills are needed in the world of work and life in general? They did not know or recognise the skills they have. I further challenged the participants by asking them to complete at least two (2) flipchart sheets of skills that they think they possess. They would often look at me in disbelief!

Whenever I finished the list, I get gasps from the participants. It blows their minds. They are in awe, when we identified and 'unearthed' the number of skills and abilities that they use in their current jobs and will need to use in their future job roles. It's a light bulb moment for them, when they realise the range and multiplicity of skills they have and especially the skills that they underutilise or never thought about.

I sometimes joke with the participants and tell them that *'they are sitting on a lot and not doing anything with it!'*

'Your skills - You are sitting on it and not using it!'

What are Skills?

A skill is the ability to do an activity or something well. A skill is what you can do. It is your ability to perform particular tasks or roles well. Being able to identify your skills is an important part of managing your life as well as change. Do you know what skills you have or need to have to move forward positively? What other skills can you apply to other areas of your life?

Our skills are usually a blend of the following:

Competencies: What can you do? What are you good at?
How effective are you? – mental, social, physical

Knowledge: What do you know and what do you not know? - organisations, services, products, people, technology, languages, legislation, policies, procedures, systems

Attitude: How do you approach things? Are you committed?
How motivated are you?

Character: What are you like? What are your qualities?
Are you a confident person? Calm?
Are you an introvert or an extravert?
Do you have a sense of humour?
Are you fun to be with?

Experience: What experience do you have? Where have you worked? What jobs have you had? Have they been paid or voluntary? What experiences do you have outside the world of work? What have you done professionally? What experience do you need?

Qualifications/ Training: What professional or vocational qualifications do you hold? What training programmes or courses have you attended? How have you developed yourself? Do you have a record of your training and development to date?
How have you been managing your learning and development to date?

Inherent Abilities: What are you naturally good at?

'I have an attitude and I know how to use it!'

You need to be able to document as well as be able to speak about your skills, abilities, knowledge and experiences in a factual manner – what you have done or achieved, without bragging! It is about getting the balance right – being positive and not sounding arrogant. The bottom line is that you must be able to communicate and present yourself well to others. Know who you are, where you are going and what you want to do rather than waiting for others to tell you.

Transferable Skills

What are transferable skills and which ones do you possess for your next job, life or career move? We all have transferable skills and need to be clear about what these are. Many of the skills that you have acquired through work and life in general can be used successfully in other areas of your life. If you are considering a move in terms of a career or doing something differently, you must examine how your existing skills match those needed in the new move/role. What skills do you need to hone in on? You will need to consider what skills you can transfer to other areas of your life. Your analysis and knowledge of your own skills will help you to better manage change effectively.

Consider the following in Terms of Identifying Your Skills:

- How is your thinking?

- What's inside of you?

- What are you good at?

- What have been your successes?

- What do you enjoy doing?

- What do other people say you are good/effective at?

- What are your personal strengths and weaknesses?

- What are your development areas or needs?

- What have been your achievements to date?

- What have been your disappointments to date?

- Have you reviewed your achievements recently? If not, why not? What are you waiting for?

- What are your specialist skills?

- What are your generalist skills?

- What skills will distinguish you from others?

Thinking of Moving On?
Consider the following:

- What is your vision?

- What is your purpose in life?

- What are your plans?

- What is your personal strategy for life?

- What are your priorities?

- What are your life goals?

- How will you create your future?

- How do you manage yourself positively?

- How do you command attention?

- What is your current position?

- Are you satisfied with your current position? If not, what are you doing about the situation?

- Is your job or role not challenging you enough?

- What changes in life would you like to make? What prevents you from making these changes?

- What would you consider to be an ideal situation?

- What is your career choice(s)?

- Do your experiences and qualities match your career choices/job roles?

- What new opportunities are there for you?

- Who is your ideal employer?

- What do you have to offer a potential employer?

- How do you present yourself to others?

- How will you improve your employability as well as earning potential?

- What professional goals have you set for yourself?

- How do you plan to achieve them?

- Are education and tradition blocking you?

- Do you feel in control of your current situation? If you are not in control, why not?

- How do you view and feel about changes, particularly in your current situation?

- What are the attributes/qualities that you will need for managing change?

- What would you like to achieve this year? And why?

- How will you make this become a reality?

- How will you reward yourself for achieving your goals?

- What do you plan to be doing in 6 months? A year? 2 - 5 years?

- What training and development would help you to achieve this?

Mirror Check:

The way you see yourself now, will determine what you become, will determine your self-esteem, your worth, your value and your importance.

'People treat you the way you see and treat yourself!'
'The boundaries that you set yourself!'

Mirror Challenge Exercise:

Keep a Mirror Diary

On a daily and/or regular basis write down your thoughts, feelings, emotions, attitudes, experiences, opinions, observations as well as ideas. Write or jot down 'things' that matter the most to you. Record and comment on events or situations. Think and write down about things quietly to yourself.

The Mirror Diary is an extension of your mind.

Mirror Challenge Exercise:

Tell Me About Me

Write 21 things about you. These are things that people do not know or would not obviously know about you.

How did you find doing this exercise?

Mirror Challenge Exercise:

Describing Yourself

Take the first letter of your first name and use the letter to think of a number of words that you could use to describe yourself i.e the words that I would use to describe me are:

- **Positive**

- **Passionate**

- **Persuasive**

- **Powerful**

How did you find doing this exercise?

Have a Mirror Moment!

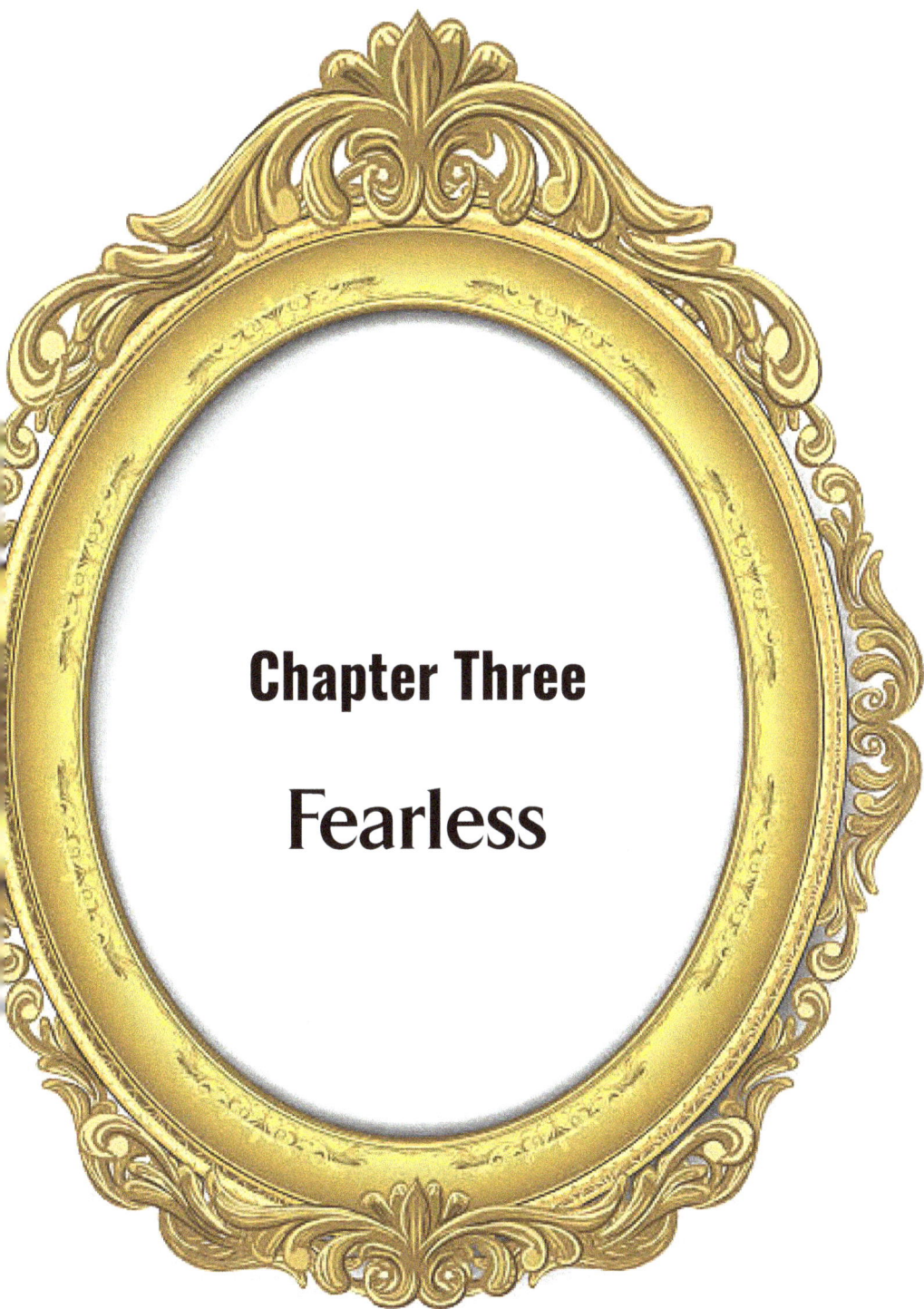

Chapter Three

Fearless

What keeps getting in the way? What holds you back? What are the main issues that you face? What stands in the way of you getting to your next level of success or moving on? Again, this is not a trick question. The answer? **You!** If you have not identified yourself, then most people identify **FEAR!**

What is fear?

Fear is a distressing emotion aroused by impending danger, evil, pain - whether the threat is real or imagined. It is the feeling or condition of being afraid. Fear is also known as a '**Phobia**'. Each of us have been a prisoner of fear at some point in our lives. There are people who are afraid of everything such as:

- Fear of heights

- Fear of space

- Fear of water

- Fear of the dark

- Fear of spiders

- Fear of public speaking

- Fear of leaving their home

- Fear of travelling

- Fear of flying

- Fear of going to work

- Fear of having no money

- Fear of having too much money

- Fear of intimacy

- Fear of relationships

- Fear of missing out

- Fear of failure

- Fear of rejection

- Fear of death

- Fear of success

How do you perceive fear?

I have come across these three meanings of fear:

- **F**orget **E**verything **A**nd **R**un
- **F**ace **E**verything **A**nd **R**ise
- **F**alse **E**vidence **A**ppearing **R**eal!

Which meaning would you chose?

Ask yourself the following questions:

- What are your deepest fears?

- What is positive/great/good (I love the word great and not good) about you?

- Are you scared?

- What are you scared of and why?

- Are you scared to do something? Make that move?

- Are you caught between a rock and a 'hard' place?

- Are you constantly challenged?

- Frightened to take the next step(s)?

- What has been or keeps holding you back?

- What makes you uncomfortable?

- Do you feel trapped in a situation?

- Do you feel that you cannot break free from a particular situation?

- Are you afraid of losing the fight?

- What is down inside of you?

- Do you seek or need approval of others and from whom?

- Are you afraid of the word 'No?'

- Are you afraid of rejection?

- How do you deal with rejection?

- How is your self-esteem/worth?

- Has your confidence been knocked or shattered?

- Is your confidence going in a downward spiral?

- What are your fears for the future?

- Do you have a compare and despair mentality?

- What would you be and who would you become if you had no fear?

Mirror Challenge Exercise:

The following features have been identified as holding us back, can you think of others?

- **Negativity**

- **Passivity**

- **Procrastination**

What does Fear do?

Fear is a dark shadow that envelopes us and ultimately imprisons us within ourselves. Fear does not stay in one place. It traps you and it holds you. Fear will torment you, shut you out. Fear will paralyse you. Pain is fear acting through the body. Fear sets in like wild fire. Fear is contagious and it spreads. Fear holds you back and locks us down. When you have fear, your senses go. It's an emotion that is crippling and doesn't help. Fear takes a grip. Fear makes you lose all hope. You feel hopeless and feelings of uncertainty about yourself creep in. Fear is the picture the enemy paints. Fear keeps bringing up your past, reminding you of your past (don't we know it). When we are afraid of circumstances and solutions, we do nothing.

Fear is the opposite of faith. Fear has got you bound. The more you fear fear, the more it finds you. As my mother would always say: 'The more you run away from something, is the more you run into it.' What you fear, you create. Don't let your fear terrorise you and force you to not take action or do something. What you say to yourself controls you and not your action(s). The things that you say to yourself (internally), have greater impact on your life than you can ever imagine as opposed to the things that you say out loud. You decide whether you want this fear to control you or not. Fear of being out of control and the need to be in control.

Sometimes fear serves limits and controls you. Fear is a spirit. Fear is a liar. Fear is an obstacle. Fear is a dream stomper and a destiny killer. Fear is jealous. Fear is insecure. Fear lacks trust. Fear lacks vision. Fear is a coward. Fear is a procrastinator. Fear is a joy stealer. Fear talks to fear. Fear is a killer!

'There is nothing wrong with having fear. It's what you do with fear that matters'

No More Fears!

The key question is: 'What is stopping you?' Our greatest obstacle is who is inside of us? The answer? '**YOU**'. Have you been crippled by fear? Are you terrorised by fear? Have feelings of fear set in? What are your challenges? Is everything moving underneath you? Are you trapped in your past? Have you felt insecure, felt useless, felt overwhelmed, felt weighed down, felt crushed and felt low down? Do you have mounting debts? Is your confidence at rock bottom following a change in your circumstances? Are you afraid that you will be exposed as a fraud? Are you suffering from the imposter syndrome, where you believe that whatever situation you are in it can't be you? It's not you. It's somebody else, it's just not you. Do you question yourself, and does this help in holding you back? Do most things petrify you? Have you always had a niggle in your head and moments of self-doubt which made you question yourself and your abilities? You need to get off the panic or the slow motion button. I keep reminding myself that I am not trapped in my past. You can't use the past to fill what's missing in the present. It is said that people with the worst past can create the best future.

Self-doubt is a common problem that can affect anyone, no matter how successful you are in life. Speaking with participants, a number of them have stated that they have not pursued their dream job or career because of fear and a lack of confidence. We live in a world where everyone is encouraged to be the best version of themselves. However, we are often stopped in our tracks by bouts of self-doubt. It's about breaking the barriers/fears that impede us from doing what we want to do. We can create possibilities that we never thought existed or imagined. Don't let anyone tell you what you can't do, especially if that person is you. We all love being in our comfort zone(s). So, stepping out of your comfort zone can be scary.

Author's Reflection

Recently I was channel hopping and caught the last ten (10) minutes of a fashion programme. What stood out for me was not the fashion/business executive having a £40 million annual turnover in terms of his business but how he got to where he is. That's what you call true guts and sheer determination. What drew my attention even more was when he questioned himself – why was he here? How did he get there? Why me? I was not qualified enough, I did not think myself good enough and I had no background in the fashion industry.

He initially felt afraid, useless, overwhelmed, an imposter and a fraud. After being kicked out of his home as well as school, he had no qualifications BUT had an idea. He further stated that he had to get on with life and the idea of failure was not an option. He was already at rock bottom, so the only way was up. He had the strength of his conviction and the courage to succeed – start and run a business – having staff, dealing with suppliers, models, social media and the fashion industry as a whole. On top of it all - making at least £1 million or more in turnover a month on just one project.

Asked what he would tell that young boy all those years ago – 'I would tell him that life is going to be okay.' Brilliant. Nothing more to be said.

'I have seen my opponent and I have no fear!'

Let's face it, it's all in the mind, your head. The first step is to recognise the problem and learn practical ways to help, overcome or manage your insecurities. It's finding ways of coping with your self-doubt and/or fending off negative thoughts and imaginations. I have learnt to acknowledge that it's fine to fail, to get things wrong. I see things as an opportunity to learn rather than a failure. Every challenge is an opportunity in disguise. I have learnt more from most challenging situations and they have made me a better and a stronger person. In life, I have seen my opponent and I have no fear. I don't allow fear to prevent me from trying, because the more you try is the more you will succeed or better prepared for the next challenge.

Are there opportunities you have passed over and things that you have restricted yourself from doing because of fear or a deep down feeling that it was not for you or it could not be you? Are we fearful of what people will or might say? Whether you do it or not – guess what? Some people will always have something to say (whether good or bad).

Be the 'cause' in your life rather than the 'effect'. Create the life that you want and control your own destiny. Dreams and fear don't go together. How do we deal with physical fear such as a fear of heights? Have you heard the saying, 'Feel the fear but do it anyway!' According to John Wayne, 'Courage is being scared enough but to saddle up anyway!' So why not climb the steps of the Shard or do a Bungee jump from 200 metres high? Are you suffering from **FOBO** – **F**ear **o**f **B**etter **O**ptions?

Are you aware that we take four options when we face fear?

1. Fight
2. Flight
3. Freeze/Frozen
4. Flow

The question is what would you do if you had no fear? That's your fear. It is suggested that one of the answers to fear is information. A number of people have fear over things that they don't even know about. Let's be honest with ourselves, our fear at times, is that we are ill-informed, misinformed and lacking knowledge and wisdom in our choices, decisions and actions that we take. Who says ignorance is bliss? That is certainly not true. What you don't know can hurt you. It is said that as adults, we have the wisdom but not the knowledge, whereas children have the knowledge but not the wisdom. I always asked participants about the best and worse scenarios and more often than not, we discuss how to deal with worse case situations. Stop having thoughts, you need to have facts. Have you lived in fear of something happening and it didn't or what if it did? There is no point dwelling on your nightmares coming true; because, even if they do, the likelihood is that they won't play out as you expect them to.

You can't keep thinking the way you did or do. Have you played it safe? Have you avoided what you thought was heartache and misery? There is a need to change your thinking; not everything is as dark as it seems. You need to overcome the fear of the unknown and confront and challenge your past. Stop running from yourself and face it all. It's your future and potential that matters, not your present circumstances. Your feelings will lie to you. Don't let your feelings rule your life. Ask yourself the question of what's inside of you and tell yourself that it needs to come out.

Reflecting on your choices is needed to move forward. Grab life by the scruff of the neck and take action! This is me preaching to me - stop having intentions and just do it. My favourite expression is 'Must Do It.' The road to hell is paved with good intentions. I often get the following responses from participants and friends that they 'will get around to it', 'must/need to look into it', 'they are meant to', 'they want to', 'they need to' and the classic, 'mean to do something'. However, 'meaning to' does not mean you are going to do it. Deal with it today. I have met so many people who say, 'I wish I had done this', 'I wish I had done so and so' or 'I should have done that/this'. As far as I am concerned, no matter your age, stage, status and lifestyle, my mantra is 'Do It', 'Do It Now'. Let's go from 'I wish I did' to 'I did it' and even further to 'I did it my way.'

'Do not give people power over you!'

Please remember that you do not need someone's permission to live. We worry too much about what other people think and say about us - it's none of our business. Am I bothered? No. Do I care? No. Do not give people the power to ruin your life. Don't let people have control over you or want to control you. I call it a manipulative and controlling spirit. Don't let people tell you how to live your life or who you should be. They are control freaks, not you. It is wrong and it is not a healthy or harmonious situation to be in. It is actually soul destroying and you are pressing the self-destruct button. Don't ever think you're powerless, it only turns you into a victim, leaving you unfulfilled in your life. Don't let people have power over you (mentally). I mean that with all sincerity.

You are your own powerhouse. Refuse to be afraid and don't allow factors such as what others think of you to get in the way of life. What others think are my disadvantage are in fact my advantage. We give our power away to people we don't even know or to people who don't even know your life. For some individuals, we have a strange way of putting our lives into other people's hands. My question is this: How can you go to people for advice, when they don't know you or have a picture of you? It's like asking someone for directions to a place, where they haven't even been themselves.

I always believe that you should never take your problems to people who have no ability to solve it. Remember your own inner voice can be your worse enemy at times. I have learnt that people will always have something to say about you - whether good or bad, whether they get permission to or not. We can't stop them from thinking or talking, but we don't have to listen to them or give them airtime, much less a sanctuary. It takes up too much of your time and energy. Anyway, what are the credentials of your critics? What do they know? They are so called 'experts' with no expertise. I have learnt that I am not subject to the Court of Public Opinion.

'You are your own powerhouse!'

It is not worth being a people pleaser. Stop being a 'POP' – 'Pleasing Other People'. People pleasing is a draining exercise. Please yourself first and more. I don't do toxic friendships. I believe in the power of association. Who do you associate with? Who do you talk to? Who are your influencers? Who are your influencers on social media? Who influences you and how? People will hurt you, but most of the time it is not intentional. What they say to you and how they behave towards you; do not internalise it, take it on board and let their actions stress you out. The human race is fickle and people are changeable like the weather. We cannot live our lives through other people and we cannot live people's lives for them. Under any circumstances, do not give people that right or privilege!

We have to learn to rise above certain things and situations and not let people affect us in every possible way. We have to be mentally tough, emotionally resilient and strong enough to not let anyone or anything break you or break you down. Remember, when you hit rock bottom the only way is up, so don't give up. It's just about you taking those first tentative steps.

Learn to focus on what matters most to you and what your needs are. Whatever you do, do it for yourself and not for someone else. We live a life we hate, because we are afraid to do something different; something new. Remember it's not about being selfish, it's about self-care. Self-care is self-worth. Do you value yourself enough to say NO? Do you value yourself enough to say YES?

'Right people energise you, Wrong people exhaust you!'

Remember, if you don't have a strong 'no', you will have a weak 'yes'. The word 'no' does not require an explanation. Read my lips, 'No' means 'No'. I have had enough of professional time wasters. I know a few. These are the people who drain and sap you of your time, energy, vitality, spirit and creativity. They drain you emotionally, physically and financially. I have not got time for drama in my life; nor kings or queens. I have enough. I have made a decision that they are not part of my circle. Remember, right people energise you and wrong people exhaust you. Don't let people's lack of support determine how far you go. Keep moving forward with or without them. I need to be around and with people who are doing something and going somewhere. It's time for you to check out or look again at your environment and surround yourself with people and things that will have a calming effect on you. Ask yourself, who makes you want to be a better person? Relationships either make or break us. We need a stabilising network of people around us. Change your circle of friends and people. We need relationships that will change our lives for the better. You need to get a team of 'architects' around you to build your life, not destroy your life.

'If you want to go fast, go alone. If you want to go far, go together!'

We have to learn to battle our fears and be more in control of our lives. Break the backbone of fear. Take authority of the spirit of fear. Be Fearless. Be Brave. Be Bold. Be unhindered. Stop being passive. Confront yourself and conquer what you confront. You have been a day dreamer too long. Get yourself out of the way or get out of your own way. Be not afraid of your deepest thoughts, fears and feelings. So what if you get it wrong? So what if you mess up? The question is, have you failed it or nailed it? Dead last is greater than did not finish. What's the biggest mistake that you can make? Not making a mistake. Not taking risks. What is a risk? Never tried it. Never done it. Is that you? Are you risk averse? Risks must be taken. I dare you to take risks.

'To be honest with you, I have said too many 'Yeses', when I should have said 'Nos!'

There is no such thing as a mistake(s), just lessons. One life lesson that I have learnt is that; 'some you win and some you learn'. Trust me, I am learning; not the hard way but the smart way. How are you going to grow or develop? I believe that sometimes things have to get worse, for them to get better. As I often say: 'If you don't go, you won't grow' or 'are you going or are you growing or 'what you sow into, you will grow into'. What do you do next? What's the worst that can happen? What do you have to lose? Was it worth taking the risk? Nothing is worse than doing nothing. Don't avoid things in life. Don't give up, don't give in. Go for it. Speak into the atmosphere and the earth will respond or project yourself and the world will receive you.

Author's Reflection

I am fascinated by the story of Thomas Edison, the inventor. As a child, his teachers said he was 'too stupid to learn anything', and he was fired from his first two employment positions for not being productive enough. This famous American is attributed with failing over 10,000 times to invent a commercially viable electric lightbulb, but he didn't give up. When asked by a newspaper reporter if he felt like a failure and if he should give up, after having gone through over 9,000 failed attempts, Edison simply stated 'Why would I feel like a failure and why would I ever give up? I now know definitely over 9,000 ways an electric lightbulb will not work. Success is almost in my grasp'.

Edison, through his failures, is also the greatest innovator of all time with 1,093 US patents to his name, along with several others in the UK, and Canada. This is truly someone who refused to ever give up no matter what.

So what if I am told 'NO'. Is that the worst that can happen? Yes, rejection does matter, it does hurt, but keep on going. Don't give up, no matter how bad the situation gets. I have learnt that 'NO' means next. 'NO' means Next Offer'. 'NO' means keep on moving. Have you felt redundant or had a shock redundancy? Have you ever felt as if you have been floored by life, and does life seem too much to bear? Failure is not final. It means further. Success is not final. Success does not have a finish line. Some people just can't handle failure; while some people can't handle success much less failure.

Failure is not failing, it's not trying anymore. It is better to try and fail than to do nothing and succeed. You never fail, until you say, 'I Quit.' Is there life beyond failure? Do things seem impossible for you to accomplish or attain? Why? Do you need a miracle? I love this - the difference between success and failure is one more time. Failure is not fatal. It is the willingness to continue that matters. Your past is your past. Let go of anger, tension, fear and failure. Remind yourself that you are not a failure. The minute you make a positive decision about your future and life, things change. You change and for the better. People use your failure to describe you, but you have a name. Have you ever achieved something as a result of failure? I have! We need to have failure, start again, create and then succeed. I have learnt and taught myself that I can't fail in life. Even if I hit rock bottom, it's only temporary and that I will bounce back. Success has been built into me. The day of failure is over.

'Success does not have a finish line!'

So what if you failed at the first, second or third time? For me '**FAIL**' means **F**irst **A**ttempt **I**n **L**earning. Failure is not an option and mediocrity is not a choice. You fail before you succeed. You fall before you walk. I have learnt that failure is not the end. The word '**END**' means **E**ffort **N**ever **D**ies. I am way ahead of those who are not trying. I have learnt that failure is an event, an education and not a person. I love this quote attributed to Thomas Edison, "I haven't failed. I have just found 10,000 ways that won't work". Don't be afraid to make mistakes. I am learning to grow through failure. It does not matter if you start wrong as long as your finish is right/strong. It is what you do and not what you have that matters. When things are not going right don't give up – just try harder. Make your focus be possibilities, be positive and resilient.

'You may have made a mistake, but you are not a mistake!

I love these questions:

How do you run a marathon? One step at a time. How do you learn a new language? One word at a time. How do you read a book? One page at a time. How do you build a house? One brick at a time. How do you change the world? One person or one life at a time. A journey of a thousand miles begins with a single step. Life is full of risks. Just breathing can be risky. What risks are you prepared to take or are you risk averse? Risks are ideas in our heads, not reality.

We take risks every day. Making choices every day. You don't get anywhere in life unless you are prepared to stick your neck out. I am learning to be fearless, big time. I love these words: 'I can see the invisible, I can do the impossible' and 'You cannot discover new oceans unless you have the courage to lose sight of the shore.'

Author's Reflection

There is a story about Evelyn and it goes like this. Evelyn was 50 years old. She thought about going back to school; being a mature student and doing a first degree. In a conversation with a colleague, she pondered that 'it would take her four years and that she would be 54 when she's finished. This is the best reply that I have heard. 'If you don't go back to school, what age will you be in four years' time?' She laughed and said, 'Point taken.' One of these days usually means none of these days.

Mirror Check:

Taking Risks

To laugh is to risk appearing the fool
To weep is to risk appearing sentimental.
To reach out is to risk involvement.
To expose feelings is to risk exposing your true self.
To place your ideas and dreams before the crowd is to risk their love.
To love is to risk being loved in return.
To live is to risk dying.
To hope is to risk despair.
To try is to risk failure.
But the greatest hazard in life is to risk nothing.
The one who risks nothing and has nothing... and finally is nothing.
He may avoid sufferings and sorrow, but he simply cannot learn, feel change, grow or love.
Chained by his certitude, he is a slave; he has forfeited his freedom.
Only the one who risks is free!

'Fear is temporary and regret is permanent'

Remember!

'Be You - The Power of You'

One way of dealing with fear is being yourself. **Be You** conscious, not people conscious. Don't try to be anyone else, but you. Be the first GREAT you and not the next best someone else. Be your own hero, actually be your own superhero. You are all you've got. There is only one of you, as everyone else is taken. There is no one like you. Try as you might – you are everywhere, so work with what you have got. By all means, admire people, be inspired by them but don't compare yourself with others. Comparison is the thief of joy. Don't become distracted.

What is the power of you? When was the last time that you felt powerful and in control? I have learnt that power is all about you – who you are, what you stand for and how you feel. It's not about how others make you feel and vice versa. Only '**You**' can make '**You**' powerful and no one else. I love the line of the song that states: 'I've got the power.' If you are looking for someone to put the power in you, look in the MIRROR. You have the power to be powerful. Being powerful is about being confident in you. It's being positive about you!

'Be your own kind of Beautiful'

'I've got the power'

A few questions for you: when was the last time you felt fearful, powerless, disempowered or run ragged? Are you under pressure to perform all the time? Have you felt messed up so much, and that there is nothing more for you? When was the last time that you made, what is considered a powerful life changing decision such as having to let go of a situation that was causing you anxiety, stress and/or burn out? There are times when we have to 'let go'. Sometimes our destiny is determined by what we let go. I am reminded of the line in a song from Frozen: 'Let it go'. The fear is not wanting to let go, as this can be terrifying. However, there is no use holding onto something that's broken, has outlived its usefulness, made you unhappy and your mind, soul and spirit is troubled or broken.

Rather than fear, say: 'Enough is enough' and make the decision to move on. I firmly believe that if you want to be different, move. Give yourself permission and have the courage to face your fears. Letting go or walking away is scary but powerful and empowering. You will be a 'better', not a 'bitter' person for it. To be honest with you, I have had to learn to let go of people, situations and things. I have made startling, but strong decisions based on my needs, where I am at and what is right for me and not on what people expect of me. I have learnt to be in total control of myself. I have an attitude that says: I have got the power to shape my own destiny, make my own decisions, steer my own pathway, take my own actions and not needing anyone's approval to do so – but my own.

I have been asking colleagues what I consider to be a simple question: 'How is work?' Their replies are interesting: 'It pays the bills', 'it's a means to an end', 'it's just a job', 'it's work' (not much more to be said), 'it's there.' 'I work because I have to and not that I want to', 'it keeps the wolves from the door'. I have even been told, 'don't ask me about work or that place.' There isn't much enthusiasm there then? Are you in a job for the sake of 'being in work (whatever it is) and that it pays the bills' and that's all that matters?

From my training experience, a number of people are not happy in their jobs. I am finding more and more people who are frustrated about work/ the jobs that they are in and life in general. What was really telling, was that people were not in fulfilling jobs and most importantly they were not passionate about their jobs/work. People are in 'limbo' in terms of the world of work. People work or they take any job that they can get or do to pay the bills. They do not really like or want to do the job that they are doing or they never thought they could do the jobs they really liked. I have realised that the problem is that many employees are in the wrong jobs and if they are being honest, they are not pursuing their dreams and passions. Basically, their passion can't pay the bills as yet.

Mirror Challenge Exercise:

Why else are you working? Are you working or living out your passion? Are you in your dream job? If not, why not? What is preventing or stopping you?

-
-
-
-
-
-
-
-
-
-

How did you find doing this exercise?

Mirror Check:

Look in the MIRROR and . . .

- Be Bold
- Be Fearless
- Be Powerful
- Be Innovative
- Be Funny
- Be Inspiring
- Be Smart
- Be Unique
- Be Yourself

Have you desperately been trying to be someone else? Are you being forced to be someone that you are not?

'Copies don't work!'

Have you ever copied someone or tried to be someone else? A number of people are having nips, tucks, botox and dermal fillers to look like someone else. According to one travel agent, people are travelling to all parts of the world for plastic surgery to get their dream body. I read horror stories of people paying thousands of pounds to have cosmetic surgery to look like some famous (so-called) celebrity or person and it did not work. My advice is that they should demand their money back. They have had cosmetic surgery and they look strange. There is a joke that a woman had had so many plastic surgery procedures that her husband no longer recognised her. As we are on the subject, another plastic surgery joke, states that two friends were meeting up after not seeing each other for some time. During the conversation, one friend says to the other: 'You look great.' To which the other replied, 'Yes, I've had a lot of work'. 'Great. Have you been exercising and dieting?' 'No, I mean I have just gotten rid of the sags, hags and bags.'

According to a Plastic Surgeon, plastic surgery is about looking fresh, not looking different. It is said that some people are seeking plastic surgery to look like their snapchat filters. There is a fear of not wanting to be seen without the filters/enhancements, should people see the 'real/true self'. My question is: Are there any real people here? Why stay in someone's shadow? Why hide behind someone else? Not even identical twins are the same. You are unique, you are enough and you are here. Stop trying to fit in and be like others. Every time you blend in you lose your identity and who you are. My question is: Why fit in, when you were born to stand out? Why conform? Go against the grain.

I remember many years ago, I wanted to have the hairstyles of certain famous persons. I went to the hairdresser and they did my hair as I had instructed or from the picture that I had shown them. However, I would look in the mirror with horror and realise a few things; either the hairstyle did not suit me or the hairdresser had not styled my hair correctly. I learnt that the hairstyle was not for me and that I needed to create my own style, my own image.

'Create your own style or image!'

Be a starter and not a follower. Be a starter and a finisher. Set the bar or trend. Don't give up on your identity and who you are. Don't give your identity to others. It is said that identity can be a giant killer in life. Have you ever photocopied a poor quality document? What were the results? The copies are even worse. Copies don't work, especially poor ones. You copied the copy. You shouldn't copy the copy or even the master copy. Be your own original. An original is worth so much more than a copy. You don't have to be one. I have learnt most importantly, to be **ME** and not a duplication of anyone else. I am unique as well as peculiar. I am happy in my own skin. I have learnt that I need to create culture, not follow culture. Don't try to be anybody else. Don't be a copy of someone else. It does not work, as it's not you. Don't try to have the same house, as your neighbour or the area will become boring. I am always reminding friends, 'let's not say copy, but you have taken inspiration from someone'.

Who is the real you? We need to be 'authentic' – real and genuine. People have got to 'feel' you before they 'hear' you. They have got to 'see' you before they 'physically see' you. It is said that people who are really liked by others is because others can see the truthfulness in them. **Be YOU**. Be comfortable with yourself. Just Be Yourself. I always remind myself that I am not where I need to be, but I am not where I use to be. I don't need to beat myself up. Stop being hard on yourself. Be your own best friend or ally. Be kinder to yourself. Love yourself; love who you are. When you look in the mirror, it's you that you see, no one else and you are the only person that you have. Don't be against yourself. Wherever you are or wherever you go you are always there. So, you might as well be great to you. You are in charge of yourself. Invent a new career; create a new you every day. I want to be the **best** me, the only me. Be yourself but only better. Make a statement. Create your own story, you don't need a ghost writer. Stand in the truth of who you are. It is what you do and not what you have that matters. When you change the way you look at things, they change your look. There is the need to find self-respect inside of you. To thine own self be true.

'Be Great to Yourself!'

The past has no life for you. Stop condemning yourself. Please stop feeling bad or sorry for yourself. Remember, when life hands you lemons, make lemonade. This quote got me thinking, that it does not have to be lemons, it can be oranges or anything that life hands you; but the bottom line is that you should deal with it. Do something with it. Another version of this saying is that: 'When life gives you lemons, make orange juice and leave the world wondering how you did it'.

Our greatest failure is our greatest turning point for our greatest success. What do you do when you see your dreams going up in smoke? You keep on having visions, even more visions. Get a vision in front of you. You see what others don't see. You see beyond the smoke. Tell yourself that: 'I am going somewhere, I will get there.' People want to put their mind set into your mind set. When people judge you, remember they are not always right. When people see you, they only see the outside of you and not the inside; not the real you. You don't want to upset others at your expense. Don't let them. Take ownership and get on with the rest of your life. Don't conform to the norm. Do great to you.

Are you a professional ostrich? Do you bury your head in the sand and refuse to acknowledge reality and what is happening around you? Do you draw back from apprehensions and impossibilities? Remember the illusion is not the reality. Perception is not reality. What you perceive on the inside may not be the same on the outside. Things are not always the same and don't assume that you will behave the same way in certain situations. It's funny how our lives can turn on a single moment or decision. One decision has the power to change everything.

'Super You'
'I know who I am. Even fear knows and stays away'

Mirror Check:

I believe in the **Power of One.**

- **One** thought can change your life forever
- **One** word can change your life forever
- **One** moment can change your life forever
- **One** action can change your performance forever
- **One** call can change your future forever
- **One** person has the power to change the world forever.

You have got the power!

'When someone says you can't do something, just say to them watch me!'

All that you need is within you. When someone says you can't do something, just say to them watch me. Don't settle for I am not educated enough, I am not good enough, I am not cool enough, I am not funny enough, I am not pretty enough or I am not smart enough. Don't settle for anything or less. Have a life changing and affirming attitude that says: 'I can' and 'I will', even when everything around you is going wrong or downhill. It's about you going against the tide of you 'can't' or 'won't'. Believing in yourself, means breaking free from self-doubt and building your self-confidence. I regularly tell people that the words 'I can't' and 'I can't be bothered' are not in my vocabulary. We as individuals have what it takes to overcome our fears and get on with our lives. Be positive and look at what you have achieved in life and not where you should be and tell yourself that you are more capable than you give yourself credit for. We must model who we say we are. A smile is the best makeup a person can wear.

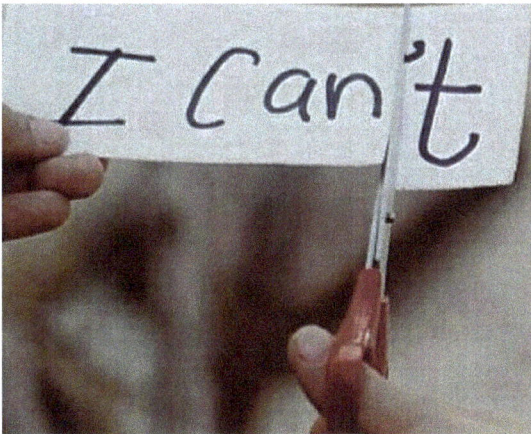

I love this quote, which states that: 'You are either part of the problem or part of the solution'. As far as I am concerned, you are the solution and not even part of the problem. If you are afraid of the circumstances, you will be afraid of the solutions. If you conceive it, you will believe it and you can achieve it. Believe in yourself and have a positive mental attitude.

Re-train your mind. Remember, nobody can tell your story like you. We need to process things differently. Have faith that you have managed your fears. Realise that you are a lot stronger today, than you were yesterday. Being connected with yourself and being the real you, are the positive signs to a 'Super You.'

Mirror Challenge Exercise:

Challenge Yourself

Rather than give up something, why not take up something? Do something that you haven't done before. Use the space below to write down 'things' you have not done before, that you would like to try/'have a go'. They can be as simple as learning to cook a new dish.

-
-
-
-
-
-
-
-
-

How did you find doing this exercise?

Mirror Challenge Exercise:

What are your 'Be Proud Statements?'

-
-
-
-
-
-
-
-
-
-

Be Proud Statements:

- Be proud of who you are

- Be proud of who you want to be

- Be proud of what you have

- Be proud of who you have become

'Stay Positive'

When something great is born, average has got to die. People can't stay in the atmosphere of greatness. Remember there are no limits, other than the ones we accept ourselves. We need to be ambitious, build our confidence and most of all gain and learn the tools that will get us back up again when we fail. Don't let your dreams be crushed to the ground. Failure, disappointments and deceit have made me bolder. The secret to success is not a secret. It's a system. The secret of success is failure. It's time to start shedding your fears and emotions. What does it feel like to push your fears, push boundaries? Be liberated, set free, get over it; whatever *IT* is. I have realised in life that it is not just the destination that matters, but the journey that I took to get there. Now is the time to reflect on your life.

- Are you living the life you were meant to be?

- Do you believe that you can do anything? Do the impossible?

- Are you optimistic when things are tough? When you are challenged?

- Are you a quitter? Give up easily?

- Is your life a one-way traffic – always going one way?

- Were you or are you a member of Dire Straits?

- Are you a risk taker?

- Are you willing to try new approaches?

Say something positive about yourself every day. Be positive when all else is falling or crumbling around you. In the face of everything, just *Stand*. I am constantly reminding participants to let their next days be their greatest days. Remember, you can't change your past, but you can change your future.

'Don't let your condition determine your position!'

Life is ten percent what you make it and ninety percent how you take it. You can work, not work, complain and remain or you can move on. We get one go in life and we need to make the most of life and opportunities given. There are no repeats; no second chances. Do whatever it is you need to do now; not later, not tomorrow, but now, while you can. Being current is the currency of life. Be a voice and not a noise. It's the decisions and choices that we make in life that determine our success and future and not money. Others may judge you, but we judge ourselves much harder. Getting through tough times builds your confidence.

'What we regret most are the chances we missed!'

Author's Reflection

I was once caught in my tracks, when I was asked the question: 'If I had a fear of success' as I had not been bold enough to undertake a number of events. The question stayed with me for some time and then I realised that it was not a fear of success but rather a fear of rejection and having to manage that!

Take a Risk

I have learnt that the greatest risk is not taking risks. I have learnt some hard lessons in dealing with failure, but not trying really gets to me. Great love and great achievements involve great risk.

Life Is Too Short

Life is short. Break the rules. Throw away the barriers. Forgive quickly. Kiss slowly. Love truly. Laugh uncontrollably, and never regret anything that made you smile!

'When the going gets tough, the tough get going!'

Mirror Challenge Exercise:

Dear Self

A Letter to Me

Write a letter to yourself about yourself

In this exercise you have to face your fears and feelings. They are real. You need to deal with them.

Dear (Here insert your name)

Love me to the stars and back.
(Insert your name)

Mirror Challenge Exercise:

A Letter to Yourself

Another variation of this exercise is to write a letter to yourself (depending on your age) from the point of view of being either a 10 year old, 15 year old or even a 20 year old.

What were/are your memories at this age?

Dear (Here insert your name)

Love me to the stars and back.

(Insert your name)

Mirror Challenge Exercise:

'Letting Go' – Purge your fears by letting go. If they are real, they can be confronted. Exorcise your Demons. What do you need to let go of?

-
-
-
-
-
-
-
-
-
-

The MIRROR Challenge   61

'In the mind is where winners are born.
Don't resort to fear.
Be Fearless.'

Have a Mirror Moment!

Chapter Four

Impact – Make an Impact!

Over the years, I have designed and delivered a number of programmes on personal/self development and more specifically examining the area of personal impact as well as personal power. I believe in the power of one. This chapter examines your personal impact and effectiveness. One of my starting point questions is asking participants to name someone that they think has great personal impact and most importantly why? What characteristics and qualities do they have? What makes this important to your personal impact? The responses that I get are very interesting and ranges from world leaders to politicians to family members.

So, what is Personal Impact? Why do participants name the late Nelson Mandela, Barack Obama or their parents as examples of great personal impact/power? What does personal impact feel, sound and look like? For me, personally, 'Impact' is about 'your presence' (your body is always speaking), your behaviour and most importantly how you 'communicate' (verbally, nonverbally and in written form) as well as how you present yourselves to others.

Personal impact is about what's on the inside of you. It is about believing in yourself and your abilities. What effect do you have on others? What behaviours do you display in certain situations? What messages and signals do you give out – present to others? Are they the ones that you intended? What influences your actions and reactions to things/life in general? How do others perceive you? How do we relate to/with others? What relationships do you have with others? Do you walk into a room and the atmosphere changes (whether great or bad)? It is about making an impact on others. The impact you make is crucial. Are you creating the impact that you want? How do we impact on each another? It is about making sure our impact is powerful and positive.

I am always asking these follow up questions to the ones above on training programmes (Looking in the MIRROR):

● What makes you, you?

● How do others see you? (parents, colleagues, family, teachers, professionals, friends and acquaintances)

● What are people seeing when they look at you? (They can be your mirrors)

● How do you project and/or present yourself?

● How do you project and/or present yourself to others?

● How and why do we communicate?

● What make you unique/special?

● What makes you different?

● What makes you stand out from others?

● How do you influence others?

● How do others feel being around you?

● How do you imagine or see success in your life?

● How can you make a difference to others?

● What are you good/great at?

● What beliefs are important to you and why?

● What are your self-limiting beliefs?

● What are your distractions?

● What are your strengths and developmental needs in terms of personal impact?

> ## Author's Reflection
>
> ### My Parents – The Biggest Influencers
>
> My parents have been my biggest and most important influencers and have had the most profound impact on me. I reflect on the wonderful parents that I had, two very different individuals with different personalities and styles of parenting. My father was a quiet and at the same time a humorous man. However, when he did speak, we had to take note. On the other hand, my mother was very talkative but a very wise woman.
>
> My mom was an entrepreneur and business woman way beyond her years and she delivered some brilliant and memorable one liners that were the best. (I still remember them today – they keep me going through the good, bad, ugly and pretty.) They worked in partnership and were great in terms of raising a family. This has had a phenomenal impact on my sisters and me, in terms of who we are as people and individuals. Whatever is your current situation, remember to make a positive and profound impact on and in someone's life. That matters immensely.

The Power of Communication

The most important aspect of personal impact and power is Communication. As the saying goes, 'We cannot but communicate and behaviour is the highest form of communication'. To be effective in whatever you do, you need to be an effective communicator. What does this mean in practice? What is Communication?

The definition of communication at its simplest, has to do with receiving and delivering messages. This can be done in a number of ways; verbal, nonverbal and through body language. Another definition given of communication - is that it is the transmission of a message or meaning, precise or vague, from one place to another. It is the transfer of information, ideas, feelings, knowledge and emotions between one individual or group of individuals and another, the basic function of which is to convey meanings.

It is an active process present in all meaningful relationships. What is the key to effective communication? Do you see yourself as an effective communicator?

The Key to Effective Communication

ME!!

'Effective, clear communication starts with each of us! It starts with me!'

Underpinning all your activities is your ability to communicate effectively with individuals, groups, peers, family and friends as well as the cultivation of effective personal and working relationships. Communication is about our experiences and you need to be aware of how you communicate.

What are the changes that you need to make in terms of your communicative style and behaviour?

'How I communicate influences my outcome!'

What are the essential Communication skills that are needed to create personal impact and power?

Identifying Your Communication Skills

Mirror Challenge - Communication Skills Exercise:

Name at least 20 Communication Skills That You Use In Creating Personal Impact and Power.

How did you find doing this exercise?

Here are some of the Communications Skills that I have thought of:

Communication Skills:

☐ Verbal communication

☐ Written communication

☐ Interpersonal

☐ Feedback

☐ Thinking

☐ Assertiveness

☐ Report writing

☐ Reflective practice

☐ Summarising

☐ People

☐ Decision making

☐ Conflict management

☐ Negotiation

☐ Body Language

☐ Listening

☐ Influential

☐ Empathy and understanding

☐ Intrapersonal

☐ Observational

☐ Recording

☐ Analytical

☐ Questioning

☐ Presentation

☐ Problem solving

☐ Review

☐ Facilitation

A much more wider and exhaustive Communication Skills list is provided at the back of this book.

Communication is based on the following six (6) Questions, which I have called 'My Six Best Friends', namely:

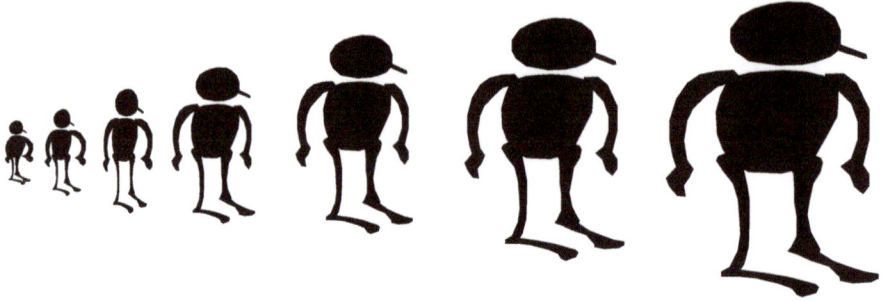

W H O

W H A T

W H Y

W H E R E

W H E N

H O W

What you say; how you say it; where you say it; when you say it; who you say it to and why you say it.

A survey conducted recently, indicated that the number one question asked is '**why**', closely followed by '**what**' and the third most popular was '**How come**?' My favourite word in the English Language is **'How'**. As a child, I would always be asking how is something done? As the popular saying goes, 'Speech is powerful'. However, it's not what you say (the words), but *how or the way you say it that counts* (tone and behaviour).

Put another way: *'It's not what you say but how you say it that matters'*. Even if someone decides not to say anything, they are still communicating. Possibly, not as how you wanted them to. Sometimes silence speaks louder than words and it is said to be golden. I have learnt that the spoken word can either encourage or discourage.

'Communication lies at the heart of all human interaction and relationships'

Communication lies at the heart of all human interaction and relationships. How you engage, interact, liaise with others, gain rapport, provide and receive feedback are important to the development of your communication style, skills and techniques and enhancing your personal impact and power. Communication is about expressing your ideas in ways that gain the attention, support and respect of others.

In communicating, words alone cannot fully express meaning. Body language, facial expression, tone of voice and other means of non-verbal communication are essential for effectiveness. Overall, when we are communicating especially face to face, these are known as the 3 V's of Communication:

V ISUAL (Body Language)
OCAL (Tone of Voice)
ERBAL (Choice of Words)

Those who study communication patterns have concluded that two-thirds of the intent of a message is communicated nonverbally (we are always communicating through our bodies), while only one-third of the message is communicated through words.

Personal impact is about communicating effectively with different types of people in a variety of situations. Effective communication is getting your message across so it is clear and simple. It's about being an assertive communicator. What does that mean? It's communicating with confidence and style. It is about establishing your credibility and demonstrating confident influential and interpersonal skills and techniques. You have the ability to look inward and to recognise your own strengths and weaknesses in terms of your personal impact/power.

Your communication with others needs to be multi-faceted. Your communication is about making a positive impact. There is the need to adapt your communication style to bring out the best in you and others. As communicators, we should always check facts carefully while being cautious about the way we share an opinion.

Communication Skills - Multi-faceted
'60 – 30 – 10' FACTOR

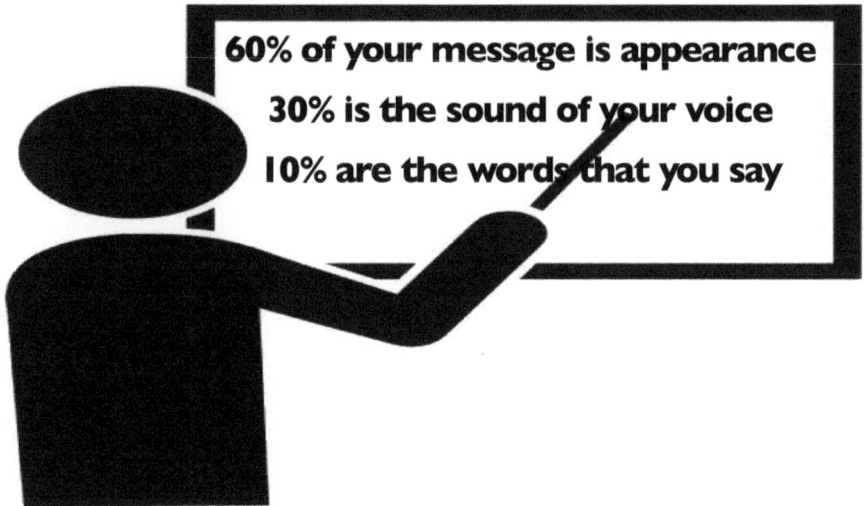

60% of your message is appearance
30% is the sound of your voice
10% are the words that you say

Verbal Communication - How are your Mouth Management Skills?

How's your language? What words and phrases do you use? One of my favourite expressions is 'Don't get me started!' How do you view life and situations? Do you choose to speak words of life or words that build up – not destroy someone or a situation? Remember, the spoken word can not only hurt or harm you, but it can kill you – your destiny and future. How does your language affect the world? How does your worth affect the world? Remember, talk is cheap and loose talk is costly. You need to watch your language. Remember, the boomerang effect, whatever we speak into the atmosphere, comes back to us or becomes self-fulfilling prophecy. On the various training programmes that I have undertaken, I have asked participants to consider the following questions when communicating verbally:

● What do you want to say?

● Who do you want to say it to?

● How do you say it?

● Why do you want to say it? What is your purpose?

● Will the other person understand?

'Check the impact of your words and most importantly how you communicate with others!'

In terms of Personal Impact and Power, participants are asked to consider the following:

- The things you say

- Where and when you say them

- Using appropriate language instead of jargons

- The appropriate media – what is best in the current situation? Is a phone call better than a series of emails being exchanged and both parties are not getting anywhere?

- Being aware of your use of diction, manner, tone, speed and volume

- Being clear and concise

- Be empathising not being patronising

- Using plain simple language and words

- Being aware of racist, sexist, homophobic or other offensive language

- Being aware of those with disabilities

- Be focused – concentrate on what you are saying

- It is probably better not to say anything than to say the wrong thing.

'Words are powerful, choose them well!'

Mirror Check:

- There is power in the spoken word

- Change the words you speak

- Your words create your world

- Get your speech right and your life will be in alignment

- What you say or speak determines who you are

- The heart is governed by words

- What you say is what you get

- You are what you say

- Put value on your words

- Words are spirit and they are life

- Speak your future into existence

- Don't use your words to describe your situation, use your words to change your situation

Body Language

Remember, we are always speaking through our bodies. So, the question is, what is your body saying? As I was often reminded by my parents, that our actions speak louder than our words. Non-verbal communication is so much more powerful than our verbal communication. As effective communicators, we need to 'set the stage' for every interaction that we have with others. People react according to their perceptions of you, which may be totally different from your intentions. How do you communicate or present yourself to others? How do you portray yourself to others in the workplace, at home, in stressful situations and in conflict situations? How do you handle awkward situations? Do you come over as weak, nervous, anxious, shy or emotional? Do you lack confidence or feel intimidated? Do you appear 'needy/begging'? Do you give off the image of the poor victim? (Why are things always happening to you?) Are you sorrow-full? Do you appear to be assertive, aggressive or even passive? Are you competent, confident and in control or are you overconfident? Are you seen as a bit of a 'show off or 'know it all'?'

'You need to check yourself before you wreck yourself'!'

You need to check your body language and how you respond to others - what signals and messages are you giving out to others? Is the message they are receiving, the one you intended? Is your mouth saying one thing, but your body is saying something else? You need to avoid sending out contradictory or confusing signals about yourself. You need to identify your personal style and how it impacts on your personal power. It has been said that for some people, we nod too much (like the nodding dog in the back of the car, if you can remember that far back). We nod when we are listening, to show that we are paying attention to what is being said. However, we should really be nodding only to show our agreement to something. It is even better if the agreement is given verbally or in writing to avoid any misunderstanding. It may also be that we talk too much and need to listen more. How can we show that we are listening effectively?

Effective Listening Skills

I am fond of the following listening skills quotes:

- 'I heard what I expected you to say and not what you actually said'.

- It's better to keep your mouth shut and be thought of as a fool, than open it and prove it!

- 'Listen as much as you talk!'

- To see the world differently, listen!

- Or as my dad would frequently ask: 'Why do you think the Good Lord gave you two ears and only one mouth?'

Are you a skilled listener? Are you listening? Do we really listen to each other? Listening is a basic need and skill common to everyone. People feel the need to be listened to. We need to talk, share ideas, attitudes, thoughts, feelings, emotions, fears and desires. In order to do so, there has to be someone who is listening. It is said, that the better the listener, the deeper the communication will be.

Listening is one of the most important, yet the most difficult and neglected skills in terms of communication and personal impact. It requires that we concentrate not only on the explicit meanings being expressed but also on the implicit meanings, the unspoken words and the undertones that are sometimes much more substantial than we think. Listening therefore requires the listener to focus all their attention and internalise the information carefully, so that their response can be more effective.

Effective listening requires that you:

- Stop talking and allow time and space for listening - you cannot listen if you are talking

- Think about what you are hearing, as you need to concentrate

- Look and act interested - show genuine interest in the other person

- Maintain eye contact throughout the conversation

- Listen and try not to anticipate what the person is saying

- Be aware of the speaker's body language. Use your eyes and ears, as words are important, but they are only the surface to what the person is actually saying or the listener needs to know

- Encourage people to talk through your body language

- Ask questions to clarify or check what the person is actually saying

- Be open minded and non-judgemental (easier said than done)

- Acknowledge what you are hearing in terms of content and feelings

- Put yourself in the speaker's position - empathise

- Not just hear the words that are spoken, but using your powers of observation

- Sitting up straight, looking and feeling alert

- Ask questions as this encourages the talker and shows that you are listening

- Stop interruptions and ensure seating is compatible to listening

- Be patient

- Remove distractions

- Listen to each other more carefully

Assertive Body Language

An interesting discussion follows with the trainees regarding their body language and the following questions emerge:

- Do you need to have feedback regarding your body language?

- How and where do you get feedback?

- What needs to change in terms of your body language?

I usually remind participants that when they are given feedback/criticism (whether they asked for it or not), or if they agree or disagree or are surprised; they should pay close attention to the 'message' been given and not the 'messenger' - the person or personality giving the feedback. People are sharing their observations and perceptions of you and with you. It's very much about not shooting the 'messenger', but examining the message/feedback given carefully (speaking from personal experiences) as well as how the message is delivered (machine).

Is there some truth to it?

This is an opportunity for you the 'receiver' to find out how your verbal or non-verbal communication skills and behaviour led to a different perception than the one you thought you had created. I am always asking participants to question themselves about how they could have done better. Could they have interacted/communicated better? Could they have used better arguments; be a stronger, more effective communicator?

What lessons can they learn from the feedback given and/or what was their behaviour/actions in terms of communicating/dealing with a particular situation as well as how would they respond in a similar or future situation. It is very much an opportunity to look at your own communication style from a different perspective, develop new insight about yourself and focus on actions and behaviours that you want to alter. I am usually encouraging participants to have a greater awareness of their own body language and how it impacts on others and most importantly what they are communicating.

Successful Communication

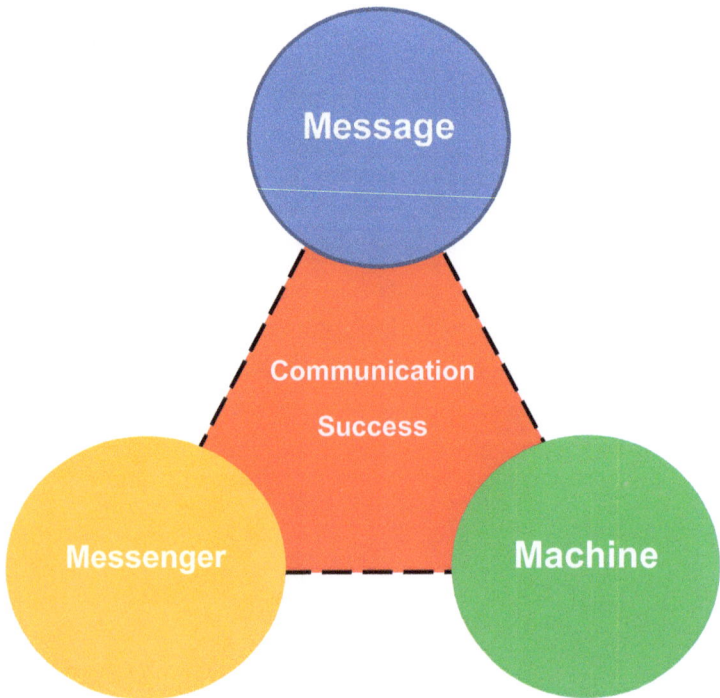

Message

Communication
Success

Messenger

Machine

'Well dressed, but still a mess!'

Author's Reflection

I was recently in a reception area when a well-dressed woman took a call on her mobile phone. The woman was obviously upset and angry with the caller and the words that came out of her mouth made my ears curl. All I could think was: Well-dressed but still a mess or as I told a friend, 'All the gear but no idea.' That's the impact she had on me.

Effective Writing Skills – 'Getting It Write'

How do you present yourself on paper? I firmly believe that the need for excellence in written communication has never been greater. This is so especially in the era of mobile phones, tablets, digital watches and technology, social media, texting and instant messaging – it makes you wonder if our writing skills have become obsolete. But, who says 'the writing's on the wall?' In spite of the social media revolution, effective writing is needed in every area of our lives. Remember, that when we are writing, we are actually speaking, so it is about getting the message/ information across with simplicity, clarity, impact and with the correct tone of voice.

I also support the old adage of 'If it's not written, it did not happen'. The ability to write effectively is an important business, work, social and personal skill but not necessarily one that comes naturally for some people. Sometimes 'putting it in writing', is easier said than done and can be a challenging exercise. I have been aware over the years of very senior officials/ members of staff who 'dreaded' writing letters, reports, minutes, reviews, summaries, documenting written evidence and/or written assessments.

Communication will only be as successful as the people who are communicating. We are being asked to express ourselves more powerfully in a variety of situations and to produce our own written communication. This requires individual proficiency and efficiency in terms of our personal impact and power and ultimately success. Let's be real; poorly written communication can have disastrous results for you, can cause anguish and a waste of time. It's not an exaggeration, if you find it difficult to express yourself in writing, your career prospects could suffer.

Your written communication must have immediate impact with your readers. We have to make it clear to the reader, so that they will not only understand, but respond in the way that we want them to. The quality of your written communication contributes greatly to the impressions that people form of you. How are your written communication skills? What is your style of writing? What does it tell a reader about you? What 'deadly sins' have you committed in your writing recently? Improving the quality of your written communication is an important part of your personal and professional development and your personal impact.

Mirror Challenge Written Communication Skills Exercise:

Make a list of your 'Rules for Writing' that you feel would make your communication most effective such as being read and understood by others.

How did you find doing this exercise?

Here are some of my 'Rules for Writing' that I have thought of:

- Plan your work out in advance – do a draft – sketch out what you want to say. Remember, Planning is the essence of effective writing.

- Effective writing requires planning, structure and the actual 'writing' comes last or at the end.

- Write in plain English.

- Keep your work short (don't be rude), keep it simple and to the point – Keep it short and simple. (**K.I.S.S rule**)

- Know the difference between spoken English and written English. As there is a tendency to write as how we speak/talk.

- Use the **'SHORT'** Rule - ***Short Words, Short Sentences and Short Paragraphs***.

- Know your readers/audience. The key question is: Will they understand you and the words/language you use?

- Avoid using initials that can confuse.

- Avoid using over complicated language.

- Be factual and accurate and avoid opinions.

- Avoid jargons, as they can lead to misunderstandings

- Choose your words carefully. Always use appropriate language. Do not use racist/sexist or other offensive language.

- Pay attention to your **GPS** - Grammar, Punctuation, Spelling, Sentencing, Paragraphs and the sequencing of information.

- Writing is actually **GPS** - Grammar, Punctuation and Spelling. Follow your GPS.

- Remember your **ABC** in writing - be Accurate, Brief and Clear.

- If possible, ask someone to proofread your work, as after a while you do not see the mistakes yourself. Take a break from your writing and allow new thoughts/thinking, also a 'refreshed' pair of eyes will spot mistakes/inaccuracies.

- Always read through your work when you have finished it and ask yourself if you have broken any of your `rules for writing'?

A list containing the Keys to Effective Writing is at the back of the book.

Think about the following:

- **Who are your readers?**

- **What are their needs?**

Remember! Remember:

Your reader may not be who you think. Anything that you write can end up anywhere – on someone's desk/computer/laptop/tablet or the Court of Law. Even the shortest and simplest written communication has this potential. Be careful what you write.

How do you want your readers to feel when they read your writing?

- Positive?
- Reassured?
- Uncomfortable?
- Excited?
- Threatened?
- Challenged?

Structure of Written Communication includes the following:

- Purpose

- Content

- Structure

- Style and Grammar

- Layout and Design

The Five C's of Written Communication include being:

- Concise

- Complete

- Clear

- Concrete

- Courteous

The Mechanics – 'GPS' – Grammar, Punctuation & Spelling

Have you ever heard of the three wise monkeys? Actually, there was a fourth, **Write No Evil** (**Grammar, Punctuation & Spelling**). We keep on leaving the fourth monkey out.

Mind Your GPS!

Remember to watch your **GPS** (**Grammar, Punctuation and Spelling**!). Grammar is the use of the rules of a language in speaking and in writing. Many people think that grammar is difficult, unimportant and write as how they speak/talk. It can be difficult at times but it certainly isn't unimportant. Grammar adds structure, logic and sense to writing. Poorly written communication can have disastrous as well as hilarious consequences for you and others (I have a growing collection of poorly worded signs and grammatical bloopers – they are priceless.) On a serious note, spelling and grammatical errors do detract from your written communication and may influence the way in which readers may perceive you as an individual, your writing and your professionalism.

Are You Always Spellbound?

How many of us can write certain words with absolute certainty that they are all spelt correctly? Misspelling can be confusing, or at the very least, distracting to the reader. Which one of these 'deadly sins' have you committed recently?

Mirror Challenge Written Communication Skills Exercise:

In your Written Communication – Spelling – which 'deadly sins' have you committed recently? Make a list.

How did you find doing this exercise?

Here is a list of 'Deadly Sins' that I have thought of:

- The use of the letter 's' in ending some words i.e. plateaus instead of plateaux, criterias instead of criteria, radiuses instead of radii

- Use the apostrophe wrongly i.e. it's for its or the boys' books for the boy's book

- Pluralise words wrongly using the apostrophe i.e. egg's, fly's, employee's, orange's

- Use 'I' instead of 'me'

- Use 'who' instead of whom

- Use 'of' instead of 'have'

- Use 'better' instead of 'best'

- Wrongly used 'am' for 'is' or 'are'

- Use of double negatives

- Got your 'ie' the wrong way around 'ei' or vice versa

- Use 'their' instead of 'there' and vice versa as well as 'they're'

- Use 'were' instead of 'where' and vice versa as well as 'we're'

- Use 'is' instead of 'are'

- Use 'was' instead of 'were' and vice versa

- Use the wrong of, off

- Did not use the hyphen properly, resign instead of re-sign

Assertiveness

Assertiveness is another crucial personal impact skill that can enhance and improve your personal power. Being assertive is a powerful communication technique aimed at influencing others and managing your behaviour. What does it mean to be Assertive? How assertive are you? For me, being assertive is knowing who you are as a person/individual. I often start with a very simple question of asking participants what their names are and the significance of their names. Again, I receive very interesting responses in terms of what people think about themselves and who they are.

I firmly believe that assertiveness is standing up for yourself and knowing what your rights, beliefs and responsibilities are, without disrespecting others' rights and beliefs. It is acquiring a positive self-image and believing that you can effectively do what's required of you. It is about being self-confident, empowered and valuing your self-worth/esteem. Assertiveness is achieving positive outcomes in life by being yourself and not letting others disempower you. It is about having a 'backbone' and using it. If you are assertive in your communication and behaviours, it means that you can maintain effective, healthy, long lasting relationships built on mutual trust and respect. People tend to value your contribution and your personal impact is even greater.

Mirror Challenge
Assertiveness Skills Exercise:

What are your rights as an individual?

I have the right to . . .

How did you find doing this exercise?

Consider your rights:

There are three kinds of Assertive behaviours, namely:

- Aggressive
- Assertive
- Passive

Having run a number of Assertiveness Skills - Personal Effectiveness and Impact Training Programmes, the following questions are asked on the courses:

- What might these behaviours look like, feel and sound like to you and others?
- What is the impact of these behaviours/communication styles on you, your personal impact and others?
- What are the benefits of being assertive?
- What should you do when communicating assertively?

What you think and feel about something will determine your behaviour/action/reaction!

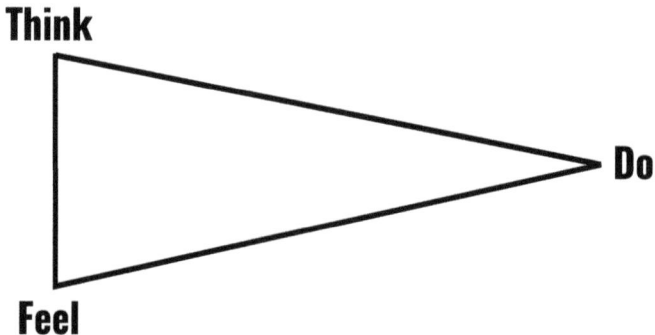

Think

Do

Feel

Your thoughts and feelings determine your behaviour/future

We even have a problem with positive language and not with negative language. How do you receive compliments? Are you gracious? Do you need to change your response/language? It is always great to accept compliments. However, some people find accepting compliments embarrassing and can be quite dismissive of them.

Author's Reflection

I have always been complimented on my skin and most of the time about my face - the smoothness, glow and beauty of my skin/my facial skin tone. I found it very difficult to accept this compliment and I would often wonder where they got that observation from? I would actually say to people, 'are you sure, are you okay?' 'We are definitely looking into different mirrors, do you need glasses or when was the last time you had your eyes tested?' As far as I was concerned – my face/skin was oily. Then I had a light bulb moment. Reality kicked in. My 'so-called oily skin' had given me that glow to my face. So, where I saw 'oily', they saw a 'glow' and smoothness to my face. Guess what? I now accept these compliments and have a laugh with friends and reply – 'I'd rather be 'greasy' than 'creasy.'

A number of issues outlined and discussed earlier in this chapter, apply to being assertive.

Assertiveness is a skill that can be learnt through applying techniques and approaches to situations to really improve your personal impact. The following tips and techniques have been given for assertive communication and behaviour and include:

- Use 'I' language/statements

- Use confident body language - I can do this! I must do this!

- Build your self confidence

- Check your feelings/body language – know when you are losing control

- Listen assertively

- Ask questions for clarification

- Be clear – know what you want

- Get your viewpoint across with clarity

- Be positive – look for positive outcomes in situations

- Meet people at their level/need, such as positioning, standing or sitting

- Know how to say 'no' graciously and several times if you have to, without feeling guilty

- Know how to give positive/constructive feedback

- Know how to receive positive/constructive feedback

- Know how to handle criticism

- Take risks

- Self-acceptance of yourself and others

- Respect yourself

- Respect others

- Self-care - look after yourself - It's the oxygen mask mentality, take care of yourself first and then others

- Celebrate your successes

'The new buzz word around here is No!'

Mirror Challenge Exercise:

Facing the MIRROR - Saying and Changing Me

As you face the MIRROR - the hardest thing sometimes is saying what you want to say. Facing what you always wanted to ask yourself.

Look in the mirror and say what you want to change about yourself.

Did you hear yourself? What do you need to change? What do you need to change in terms of your communication skills and techniques?

What do you want to change in terms of your behaviour?

Next time choose someone you trust and say what you want to change about yourself to them.

'Tell the truth and shame the devil!'

Mirror Check:

Remember:

- You need to understand the impact you have and what the mirror is telling you

- To build your confidence, embrace and enhance who you are

- Confidence is how you look and feel about yourself

- Not to judge yourself too harshly. Some people will (judge you), some won't. So what?

- Don't let your own inner voice become your worse enemy

- Show your inner strength and power – believe in the power of one!

- You have a voice and you need to use it!

- The more you let people in, is the more they get to know you

- Stop worrying about what other people think and say about you

- Forget about social media and don't live your life through it

- To ask for feedback to identify your strengths and development areas in terms of your own personal impact and power

'We all carry scars, inside and out. It's how you wear them that matters!'

Mirror Check:

Play on Words – Your Choice of Words

- Get wisdom, get understanding.

- Know wisdom, no wisdom

- Know understanding, no understanding!

- You are not a cook, until you cook!

- If you go right you are wrong, if you go left you are right!

- If you stay ready, you don't have to get ready!

- Is it a blank cheque or a bad cheque?

- They can who believe they can

- Loving what I do and doing what I love

- Know what they like and like what they know

- To keep moving, you have to keep moving!

- If you don't know, you won't know!

- Eat to live or live to eat?

- You cannot manage time, time will manage you!

- Very bad at being good and very good at being bad!

- I thought your idea to use my idea was a great idea!

- Use your insight to overcome your oversight!

- It's either knives in the back or a pat on the back!

- Knowledge is knowing what to say. Wisdom is knowing when to say it!

- Do the right things to make the right things happen to you!

- All good things must come to an end but who knows when?

- Love the life you live, live the life you love

- There are no potholes, but road in the holes!

- If we do not plan for the future, we will not have a future! We plan for no future!

- It's not about what you are eating, it's about what's eating you?

- To seize the opportunity of a lifetime, you have to do it within the lifetime of the opportunity!

The trouble with writing:

- A man receives a cheque which says, 'Don't cash this cheque until I tell you!' He's still waiting!

Author's Reflection

Think on These Things.

- You have a quality that is not in books.

- What you believe of yourself, the world will believe as well.

- How far you go depends on where you start.

- If not now, when?

- A listening heart and a hearing mind.

- Wisdom takes time. Knowledge is instant.

- Your face is your future and your back is your past.

- I do know the answer but not to that question.

- You haven't asked me the question, but here is the answer.

- To get the rainbow, you have got to get the rain.

- You know what you have, you never know what you are going to get.

- The race is not always for the swift...but for those who keep on running.

- Your talent gives you entry, but it's your character that gives you staying power; or said another way, charisma takes you there and character keeps you there.

- The grass is not always greener on the other side; it's how you water it that counts.

- Due to operational and financial difficulties, as of tomorrow, the light at the end of the tunnel will be switched off until further notice.

Have a Mirror Moment!

Chapter Five

Reflect – The Mirror is Your Reflection of You

'The Mirror said Reflect before you act'

You have to clean the mirror, to get a true reflection of yourself!

Who do you think you are?

The first '**R**' in the MIRROR is to reflect. Looking at your reflection, the obvious question is who are you? Who defines you? What defines you? As a facilitator on numerous training courses and workshops, as part of the ice breaker exercise, I usually ask participants to describe themselves as either a fruit, vegetable, ice cream, drink, biscuit, cartoon character or work of art and most importantly why they have made this choice. This exercise really does break the ice. It's quite interesting, hearing people's choices and how they have responded and there is such hilarity when they say why they have made such choices. I should write a book on that alone.

So, the question is who are you? Who are you when no one is looking? Who are you not? What are your thoughts about you? Why do you do what you do? How have you been over the years? What's going on in you? What are you expecting in or from life? What are your motives for doing things? Is being yourself an occupational hazard? Have you lost sight of who you are? Are you invisible? I love these two songs, 'I know who I am' and 'I am what I am'. Who is the real you? What's your identity? Is it a case of mistaken or stolen identity? What's your culture and background? I am fascinated by the television programme, '**Who do you think you are?**' What has your DNA told you about you? Your DNA makes you who you are. The DNA that's in you, no one has it. Who are your family and who are you connected to? Where are you coming from? What part of the world does your DNA originate from? What is the composition of your genetic make-up? I usually joke with family and friends and say, 'I have traced my family tree, so I know who to blame. Remember in every family there is a sap.

Are you hiding behind a mask or is the mask slipping? Take your mask off. When you live in your mask, you stay in fear. The mask makes us weak. Where are you now and where do you want to be? Finding out who you are, is a journey of self-discovery. What has or have been the turning point(s) in your life? What challenges have you overcome? How many knots do you need to untie to reveal the real you? How much of yourself have you compromised? Has your worst nightmare become a reality? Most importantly, what have you discovered about yourself? What do you like and don't like? (We are not talking social media here.) Are you doing things on your own terms and with your own voice? A voice that many times we have told ourselves is less important or relevant than someone else's. We need to re-frame the situation. We need to break free from our chains.

You have got to tell yourself who you really are and not let someone else tell you. No one can beat you being you. Do you ever feel the true you is hidden, even from you and that it needs to come out? Life does not give us what we want, it gives us who we are. Does society or do we confine ourselves to boxes, forms or labels? As far as I am concerned, I am not in a box and I cannot be put in one. Labels are for boxes and bottles, not people. I am often reminding people to think outside the box or form. Don't get pigeon-holed in their thinking. I am aware of colleagues who have been told as children and young people and this could still be the case that they should not apply to study certain subjects at particular universities, as 'they won't get in', 'no one has ever got in' or 'you won't become the next Prime Minister' and they were given 'alternative' career choices/options. I have also spoken with colleagues and friends who have not applied for jobs outside of their areas of work (although they have shown interest or a passion) for fear of rejection or being judged by others. Don't let society and people place limitations on you and what you can achieve.

'Be your own cheerleader and the loudest one!'

The Importance of Reflection

According to the Oxford Reference Dictionary, the word 'reflect' in terms of a mirror means 'to show an image of' or 'something that comes back to you'. The other meaning that I am fond of 'is to think deeply, to consider, to remind oneself of past events'. So, if you look in the mirror, you will see your *reflected* image. If you *reflect* on your past experiences, you look at them thoughtfully. Reflection also means 'the use or exercise of the mind or one's power of reason in order to make inferences, decisions, or arrive at a solution or judgements'. Reflection is a form of mental processing and it causes you to think. It allows you to improve your thinking. It's about having a greater understanding of who you are. Reflection is peeling back the layers of your life. Every one of us has got a demon – something that we go back to. Even superman had his demon – Kryptonite. We go back to our past, when we are challenged. When we are being attacked, we go to past habits/situations that are wrong for us. What are you reflecting on? We reflect on a whole host of issues – it's called life in general. As the saying goes, 'No experience, No reflection'.

'No experience, No reflection'

Reflection helps to turn your experiences into learning. What have you learnt or what are you learning? One of the areas that I undertake with participants over the years is 'Reflective Practice'. What does Reflective Practice involve? It is what it says on the tin – reflecting on your practice, your work and how you do things/handle situations. Reflective practice involves thoughtfully considering and critically analysing your actions and own experiences with the goal of improving your practice. It is about making time for you to reflect on what you have learnt in particular situations and includes the following:

- Revisiting your experiences/past

- Analysing what was/has been happening

- Identifying behaviours, ideas, thoughts, feelings and actions

- Assessing your strengths and development areas

- Exploring positive and negative aspects of your life

- Examining ways of moving from negative to positive

- Affirming the positives in your life – taking you to your next level

This chapter is about getting you to reflect on you. It contains a number of reflective exercises that you can do, to check where you are currently. Writing down reflections and your self-assessment will help you to consolidate your thinking. There are no right or wrong answers. It is not about you (mentally) 'blaming or beating yourself up,' but it's about you being honest with yourself and your situation and what changes you need to make in terms of going forward.

Reflective practice requires you to:

- Have an experience

- Review the experience

- Conclude from it and then

- Plan the next steps

Another way of looking at Reflective Practice is that you:

● Plan - Plan the activity

● Do - Perform the activity

● Check - What was the outcome of the activity?

● Act - Act on the information from the activity

Keep going around the circle until the activity cannot be refined or improved in any way.

Reflective Practice Tips, Tools and Techniques:

The following list highlights some reflective practice processes that may be helpful:

● Asking the who, what, why, where, when and how questions (My Six Best Friends)

● Questioning what, why and how you do things

● Questioning what, why and how others do things

● Comparing and contrasting

● Seeking alternatives/options to what you do

● Keeping an open mind

● Being honest with self, not defending

● Examining a rationale or framework as to why you do things

- Viewing things from other people's perspective/position – have you heard the saying, 'There are three sides to everything; your side, my side and the other side.'

- Asking 'What if?' questions

- Asking 'So what?' questions

- Asking 'how would you do things differently?'

- Asking others for their ideas, viewpoints and differences in opinions

- Considering choices and decisions

- Considering and weighing up the consequences of the decisions you make

- 'Chunking/breaking up' information and things

- 'Chunking up' – moving from the specific to general (why?) and 'chunking down' – moving to specifics (how?)

- Testing and trying out theories and beliefs

- Identifying and resolving problems

Can you think of others?

'There are three sides to everything: your side, my side and the other side!'

Looking in the Mirror – How about undertaking a 'selfie' of a different kind? Actually, the MIRROR Challenge starts with a period of personal reflection. Take time to ask yourself some key searching and thought-provoking questions – a self-review/analysis and write down the answers. The questions include:

- What are you thinking?

- Where are you now?

- What's inside?

- What plans have you made for yourself?

- What's your vision of you?

- What's your future?

- What do you want to do?

- What do you need to do to get there?

- Where do you want to be/go?

- What have you got to offer?

- What skills and abilities have you not yet fully utilised?

- What do you need to improve about yourself?

- What do you need to change about yourself?

- What do you need to change around you?

- What are your beliefs?

- What are your dreams?

- What are your destiny killers?

- What issues do you need to leave behind?

- What is your purpose in your life?

- How are you going to get there?

- What's your personal brand?

- What is the big picture? Where do you fit in?

- What are your aims and goals in life?

- How do you plan to achieve your goals?

- Have you achieved your goals and objectives? If No, Why not? If Yes, How?

- What existing resources (attitudes, beliefs, capabilities and skills) do you have?

- What have been your achievements?

- What motivates you?

- Who or what are your motivators?

- Are you driven to great heights? If not, why not?

- Are you confident with yourself?

- What is holding you back from progressing/achieving?

- What are or have been your barriers and obstacles in your life?

- What makes you uncomfortable?

- Are you your own obstacle?

- How can you overcome these?

- Have you exceeded your limitations? Dreams? Aspirations?

- What are you passionate about?

- What personal activities have you engaged in during the past year that you are proud of?

- What was the impact of this activity on your life?

- Who do you trust?

- Who speaks to you and most importantly what are they saying?

- Who do you associate with?

- Whose wings are you under?

- Who do you listen to?

- Who influences you?

- What drives you?

- What do you celebrate?

- What things grab your attention?

- What are you giving your time to?

- Are you in control?

- Are you controlling what you need/want to control?

- Have you created your own future? If not, why not?

- How do you make a difference?

- What can you do differently from others?

- What aspect of your life satisfies you the most and the least?

- Do you run away from your reflection in the mirror?

- What are you afraid of?

'When you looked at your reflection in the mirror, did you have a moment(s)?'

> ### *Mirror Challenge*
> ### *'Reflection' Exercise:*
>
> ## Challenge yourself to take a DNA Test. It's worth it. (Find out more about yourself)

How did you find doing this exercise?

There are a number of reflective exercises that can be undertaken, here are a few.

Mirror Challenge 'Reflection' Exercise:

A Message to My Future Self

What is the Message?

How did you find doing this exercise?

***Mirror Challenge
'Reflection' Exercise:***

If you could go back in time, what advice would you give to your younger self and why?

How did you find doing this exercise?

Mirror Challenge
'Reflection' Exercise:

What is your bucket list? What would you write on your Bucket List?

How did you find doing this exercise?

Mirror Challenge
'Reflection' Exercise:

Write down 20 things that you want or need to achieve before you leave this earth.

How did you find doing this exercise?

Mirror Challenge
'Reflection' Exercise:

What have been the positive and negative experiences in your life?

How did you find doing this exercise?

Mirror Challenge
'Reflection' Exercise:

Some things I could have learnt to do better...?

How did you find doing this exercise?

Mirror Challenge 'Reflection' Exercise:

I remember...

Close your eyes and think about the things you remember fondly.

How did you find doing this exercise?

Mirror Challenge
'Reflection' Exercise:

The Rumours

The rumours are true . . . . What are the rumours?

Think and write down words that best describe you.

I am . . . .

How did you find doing this exercise?

SCOT Analysis

Have you heard of the **S**trengths, **W**eaknesses, **O**pportunities and **T**hreats (**SWOT**) Analysis? How about doing a **SCOT Analysis** on yourself?

Strengths	Challenges
Opportunities	Trials

I have been discussing with colleagues and friends recently birthdays and especially birthdays ending in zeros. This has got me thinking and reflecting about life and in particularly life lessons or 'grey advice' as I call it. Sometime ago, for a significant birthday and during a period of quiet reflection, I wrote down lessons I have learnt in life. What are/have been your significant lessons in life? Part of looking in the MIRROR is looking back - lessons learnt from our past and experiences, which should prepare us for the future – however, for some of us this can also be painful. Some years ago, I challenged myself to write '**Laws of Confession and Declaration Statements**' – with every statement beginning with, '**I am so grateful that . . .** '. I wrote over eighty (80) statements and found the exercise quite therapeutic, challenging, as well as refreshing.

Mirror Challenge 'Reflection' Exercise:

An Attitude of Gratitude

'I am so grateful that . . . '

What are you grateful for? Just what are you thankful for? Write statements beginning with 'I am so grateful that . . . '. Challenge yourself to write as many as you can.

How did you find doing this exercise?

Mirror Challenge
'Reflection' Exercise:

What significant lessons have you learnt in life?

How have these changed or moulded you?

How did you find doing this exercise?

**Mirror Challenge
'Reflection' Exercise:**

Exercise: You

What would you call the story of your life?

Exercise: You

In the story of your life - what would you call one of the chapters in your book?

How did you find doing this exercise?

Here are some of my life lessons or 'grey advice':

- Life Happens.

- I own who I am.

- Become the one.

- Be a name, not a number or statistic.

- Make a statement.

- Appreciate the simple things in life.

- Appreciate what you have.

- I love simplicity.

- Do it with your mind! Not my mind.

- Go for what you want.

- Success has been built into me.

- I am a prophet of my own life.

- You can't do better until you know better.

- I am better, not bitter! Life's too short.

- Life's too short so make the most of it! Be happy.

- Out of every bad situation comes good.

- Language is powerful.

- If you don't ask – you don't get.

- Don't be confined or defined by anybody.

- No man is an island.

- I have learnt to develop a thick skin and a tender heart.

- To be kind and encouraging to myself.

- Be kind but don't let people abuse you.

- I have learnt to go where I am celebrated and not where I am tolerated.

- I have learnt that where my kindness, generosity, compassion, help and support is thankfully received and reciprocated, that's where I am.

- You have to start somewhere, before you can get anywhere.

- If you don't move forward you will always be at the same place.

- For some people to move, we have to push them.

- The best way to learn something is to do it.

- Be bold, be brave and be different.

- Passivity leads to inactivity.

- Don't apologise to people that don't know you.

- You can't do everything but you can do something.

- If I give up, I will never get up.

- Do not give up. The beginning is always the hardest.

- Take pride in how far you have come. Have faith in how far you can go.

- It's never too late to start again.

- If you don't choose your future, someone else will.

- Perfection does not exist, so stop striving for it.

- Practice makes permanent.

- Be content but never stop improving on yourself.

- Plan for the future.

- Material things do not matter.

- Trust your gut instincts.

- Trust but don't be deceived.

- We choose what we carry – the baggage and the weight.

- Absence makes a statement.

- See life differently, live life differently.

- Create your own platform.

- Always embrace the unexpected.

- Haters are elevators to your life.

- Do not to confuse stubbornness with strength.

- If you don't prioritise your life, someone or something will prioritise it for you.

- Whatever happens to you in life, it means you must journey some more.

- Life is ten percent what you make it and ninety percent how you take it.

- Never hate your enemy, as it impacts your judgement.

- Pain has been my counsellor, life has been my teacher.

- Cherish happy moments and time spent together.

- Take off the blindfold and enjoy today.

- Live life one day at a time.

- Live your best life.

- Live life on your terms and no one else's.

- Some lessons are painful; some are painless but all are priceless.

- Love unconditionally.

- Forgive abundantly.

- Enjoy life.

Recently, I attended a retreat where the tranquil setting of peaceful and secluded gardens provided a place to think and listen to the hushed sounds of nature and to my own thoughts.

The retreat also provided the opportunity for spiritual direction, renewal and personal reflection.

I love this quote:

'The best therapy does not always require an appointment!'

Author's Reflection

It's worth experiencing the healing powers of nature.

Remember:

- Guilt, grief and pain are concerned with the past
- Worry and stress are concerned with the future
- Contentment, gratitude and peace are concerned with the present

Mirror Check:

- Feel confident with the person looking back at you.
- Know who you are.
- Know whose you are.
- Know your DNA.
- Know your family, your roots and where you are from.
- Know where you are.
- Be true to you.
- Reflect on your choices and decisions.
- Confront your past.
- Deal with today.
- Hope for tomorrow.
- Reflection . . . Moments . . . Take today and live the moment.
- Live your life with integrity – like no one is watching.
- Make today the best day of your life.

Have a Mirror Moment!

Chapter Six

Respond – Take Action!

The second '**R**' in the MIRROR is to respond, to take action. According to Booker T. Washington, 'The circumstances that surround a person's life are not important. How that person responds to those circumstances is important. The response is the ultimate determining factor between success and failure'. Put another way: It's not the circumstances that are so damaging to you, it's your reaction to them. Even in situations where you have no control over events, you can still choose your reaction. At times we do moan and complain and feel sorry for ourselves, however, the key is how quickly you snap out of it. I firmly believe that we are not to complain about something that we are not prepared to do something about. Complain, but have a vision. There is a popular saying: 'Actions speak louder than words'. We need to be looking at what people do rather than what they say.

'Don't wait, just activate!'

There is a saying, 'You are the holder of your destiny'. You are the architect of your future. We are constantly battling for our future. So, do something. Make it happen. As the saying goes, 'Life is 10% what you make it and 90% how you fake it. If you don't do something, it's not going to get done. Act, react and take action. We fall short of NOT taking action. We say things, but don't do them and never follow through (guilty as charged). The MIRROR Challenge wants you to look in the mirror and take action. There are mirrors everywhere. The key to life is taking action – prior to taking action is making a decision. Are you timid at making the right decisions? Your actions must be based on your character and not on your emotions. It is your will in all things. Take those critical steps. Look at yourself and make those adjustments, changes, but most of all take action. The question isn't can you? It is will you? As the saying goes: 'The smallest adjustments can make the biggest difference. Take action to what you have heard and learnt. When you believe something, start acting on it. People want action. Watching a television (TV) detective show, the Inspector said to the detectives: 'I don't want words, excuses or theories, I want action!' 'Find the culprit!'

A Call to Action!

Looking in the Mirror, Questions to ask yourself:

I have found that asking questions, places you in control.

- How do you need to respond?

- What action do you need to take?

- What do you need to do?

- What are the possibilities?

- What are the options?

- What are the risks?

- How are you going to do it?

- What will you need?

'Act so you don't have to react!'

As my mother would say: 'Do something, before something happens to you'. Take action on your dream(s). Stop the excuses. Death to excuses. No more excuses. Enough is enough. What's the problem? We have so many opportunities around us. Re-engineer yourself, re-design yourself and stop deceiving yourself. Wake up. Get up and get it done. Just do it. Stop putting things off. Just make a start and get on with it. The atmosphere you create will determine what you produce. The difference between goals and achievement is action. Stop making decisions based on assumptions. Difficult choices tell us more about who we are and what we are really made of. You get one go in life, so you need to take it. Do you want to be stretched? Do you want to be challenged? Taking action means moving on.

'Take your destiny by force!'

So, where do we start?

The Power of Your Mind

Responding - taking action begins in the mind. Who we are begins in the mind. It is said that the biggest problem with mankind is our thinking. The mind is the centre of our reasoning. I have learnt that the mind can be a dangerous place to be. The mind is the ability to think. It is a powerhouse. Humans have the power to think, create, produce as well as change their minds. Thoughts and dreams are the foundation of our being. Your mind remembers and your mind imagines. It is your memory and your imagination. It is your past and it is your future. Where are you right now in terms of your thoughts and thinking? What is your thinking like? Where is your head? Where are your thoughts resting/set? What goes on in your head/imagination? Everything starts and ends within the mind. Are you stronger than you think or look? Our mind is where we live our lives. Many of us, live in the closet of our past. You can either agree or ruin your thoughts, which determines your reality. It is your reality that defines you.

'Your mind remembers and your mind imagines!'

Your mind is set. Hence the word 'mind-set'. What is your mind set on? I have learnt that I am a product of my thinking. The mind can be challenging, hence it's a battleground or field. There is always a battle going on in our minds. The warfare is in your head. Your mind is your greatest enemy and leaving you alone with it, creates problems. The greatest gift that I can give a person is for them to change their mind. Think differently and then act differently. You can be or do anything you want to as long as you put your mind to it. Is it time for a new mind-set, a new perspective on life?

Success begins in the mind. Limits only exist in the mind. Your mind can create many impossibilities that build up barriers in your life, which leads to limitations. However, life does not have to be this way. Say no more to impossibilities. The sky is the limit, if you let it be. As the saying goes, 'So a man thinketh so is he.' There is nothing more powerful than a made-up mind. A mind that is empty; goes anywhere, is led anywhere. Whereas, an occupied mind is not deterred. It is focused and not easily led.

Change your mentality and your thinking and you will have a brand new you. Think yourself to wherever you are going/want to go, as your mind already sees where you are going. Your feelings follow your thoughts. If you can deal with your headspace, then you can deal with life and the future. You are in control of your every thought. Re-arrange your thoughts and don't let them push you around. Push your thoughts around. So, remember the positives, the victories, the gains, achievements, breakthroughs and successes and do not dwell on the negatives. Give your mind an imagination to pursue.

'Your mentality determines your reality!'

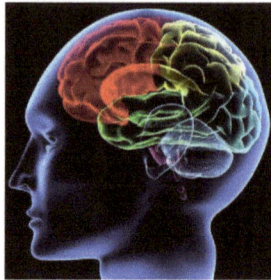

'The mind is a terrible thing to waste!'

$$\frac{MIND}{MATTER}$$

If you don't mind, I don't matter.

If I don't mind, you don't matter

Those who mind matter

Those who don't matter, don't mind.

The Mind Boggles

- What's on your mind?

- What is the condition of your mind?

- What is your greatest thinking?

- What do you do with your thoughts?

- Are you happy and contented?

- Are you scared with what you see?

One of my popular sayings on training is: 'I want your mind' to which the participants respond 'that I can't have it, not even a piece.' All human transactions begin with a thought. What are your thoughts? What do you think about? Only you can control how you think and act and no one else. Have you talked yourself out of something? Have you talked your future away? Have you talked your happiness away? Wherever you end up, is down to you. Changing your mind means that you change your thoughts, your speech and ultimately your actions. Think it and speak it.

What's going on in your head? How do you process life? Do you believe you can do anything? Are you optimistic when things are tough? Do you feel that you are in a sea of despair? Been on an impossible journey? Are you ready to quit/give up? Many of us are crippled with self-doubt and confidence. It has been stated that the reason why people are not able to accomplish their goals is the lack of self-confidence/esteem.

I call some of our negative thoughts **'Stinking Thinking'** or **'Toxic Thoughts'**. In your mind set, you have already defeated yourself before you have even got started. Wrong thinking mind-set is powerful. It affects our behaviour and our progress in and through life. We have old mind sets and ways of working, that we need to let go. Aspects of your mind seek to predict, control and avoid pain. A lot of people **DO** a lot, but **THINK** little. Think is your action. Your mind is always working. It is the centre of your creativity. You think what you become. You need to mediate, day and night. Most people use very little of their mind power. Have you heard the saying: 'Success is easy, so is neglect'? Many of us, do nothing, we choose – reject and neglect. Neglecting the development of your mind is dangerous. Never stop growing your mind. If you are not working on yourself, you are not working. Many times, I marvel at the wonders of creation and the power of man to invent and build. Think positively and grow your mind.

'Your mind is a powerhouse!'

Most of us live a habitual, day to day existence, doing the same things over and over. We are creatures of habits, like robots. Lots of things are happening around us, which I call background music, but don't get too caught up in it. Remember, you need to check yourself before you wreck yourself. You can't change the past, but you can certainly ruin the present by worrying about the future. Who or what influences you? Who are your role models? They can influence us greatly and they will shape the way that we see and view the world and life.

'Sharpen your mind!'

We need to change. I believe some of us need a mind transplant. A lifestyle overhaul. There needs to be a shift in our thinking – a paradigm shift. We need to think and do things differently. We need to shift the 'who, what, why, where, when and how' thinking. We need a mind-set change in terms of our choices, decisions, behaviour and ultimately our actions. Changing the way you think will alter the way that you deal with life's challenges and the *'false'* limitations that you place on yourself. Your mind needs mental exercise just like your body needs physical exercise. Sharpen your mind. Please don't lose your mind, use your mind. Use your mind to create, produce, invent, review and problem solve rather than 'sing the blues'. Change your thinking and your thinking will change what's happening/ going on around you. Remember, it's a state of mind and you already have it.

'You can either choose, to use it or lose!'

I have come to realise that your mind is an amazing and intricate computer system. Your mind is the most important feature of you and is your greatest investment. What investment are you prepared to make in terms of your mind, thoughts, thinking and ultimately the actions you take? Invest in your mind. Invest in your life. I don't know about you, but I invest in books, CDs, DVDs and a variety of media platforms to stimulate my mind and most importantly to learn from people, their lives and experiences. It is said that reading is to the mind what exercise is to the body. I believe it's much better to read it than to have lived it.

Your mind determines or destroys your future. Your mind either talks you into or out of something. You are both the holder and participant of your destiny. Is your mind open to receive, open to change? We get placed into certain situations for us to change our mind set as well as to grow. You have got to believe it to be in it. You have got to conceive it to achieve it. I have learnt that your mind needs a focus and needs to be mastered. Choose your focus. Try to keep your focus – easier said than done. Give your mind an assignment. It is said that, broken focus kills every dream. The law of focus eliminates distraction. Get interested in your talents, hobbies and projects as well as in personal growth activities. You have got to renew, refresh, transform your mind and have a new focus. I consider myself to be a lifelong learner, so I am always learning.

'Get your mind off yourself!'

I love this powerful and inspired piece of poetry – '***Thinking***' by Walter D. Wintle. It echoes deep in the recesses of my mind. The poet is best known for writing this world famous poem.

Mirror Check:

'Thinking'

If you think you are beaten, you are!
If you think you are not, you won't
If you like to win but don't think you can
It's almost a synch you won't

If you think you will loose, then you've lost!
For out in the world you will find
Success begins with the person's will
It's all in the state of mind

If you think you're outclassed, you are!
You've got to think higher to rise
You've got to be sure of yourself
Before you can win the prize

Think big and your deeds will grow
Think small and you'll fall behind
Think that you can and you will
It's all in the state of mind

Walter D. Wintle

Author's Reflection

An attitude is an outward reflection of a thought life.

Great minds don't think alike… They think creatively,
they challenge current thinking.

I am not afraid of tomorrow. I have seen yesterday and
I love today.

If you fill your heart with regrets of yesterday and the worries of
tomorrow, you have no today to be thankful for.

Tomorrow hopes we have learnt from today.

Potential – What's your potential?

Potential is hidden ability. It's already in you. You are full of potential. We are all born with potential. Potential has no limits, it's what it becomes that matters. The question is: How do we harness this potential? Life is about you achieving your potential and maximising your opportunities. Potential is not based on what you have done, but what you have not done. It's your future potential that matters not your present circumstances, so focus on the present. Your potential is not known until you make a demand on it.

Knowing what you want

One of my favourite sayings is 'If you don't ask, you don't get. We are being told to ask for what we want. However, I have found that many people have a problem with this. They don't *KNOW* what they want. Do you know what you want, what you really want in life? It reminds me of the Spice Girls song – 'I'll tell you what I want, what I really really want'. The reality is that you can't ask for what you want unless you know what it is.

Be Prepared

The **three key words** for effective living are:

- **Preparation**
- **Preparation**
- **Preparation**

I use to be a senior Girl Guide and the motto for the Girl Guides is 'Be Prepared'. How prepared are you when the challenges, storms, winds and rain come along in your life? How prepared are you to deal with redundancy, retirement or losing your job, a contract or the loss of a loved one? What do you do next? What does being prepared mean? I recently watched a television programme where company directors spoke about the future of their businesses. Interestingly, one director said they were preparing for the next five years. However, another director said that they were not just looking ahead for the next five years, but fifty years. Talk about being prepared. That blew me away. The diligent prepare for opportunities that don't exist. It's about being prepared and planning ahead. Be diligent about what you do. You need to be fully prepared.

'You can't predict the future but you can prepare for it!'

Being Prepared - Planning

Some of my favourite quotes on planning include the following:

- No plan, no destination
- The proof of your future is in your plan
- You failed to plan because you planned to fail

- Poor planning on your part does not constitute an emergency on my part or said another way - an absence of forward planning on your part does not constitute a crisis on my part!

- Poor planning and poor preparation produces poor performance

- An idea without a plan, is just a dream

- Tomorrow's success is determined by the people behind today's plans

So, how much of your life can you plan? As the saying goes: 'I don't expect success, I prepare for it'. How do we prepare ourselves? Firstly, we need to make and maintain plans. Have you ever observed or watched Olympians and top class athletes, footballers, rugby players – they are constantly practicing. Their aim is to win games and to do so, they are either playing or practicing. They prepare or practice in and out of season as well as for the next season. They make plans and are prepared to win. Preparation is never time wasting.

Planning needs to be part of our routine, whether it is hourly, daily, weekly, monthly or yearly, but we need to plan or have some form of planning. It is the process and practice of setting goals, developing strategies and ideas, outlining tasks and schedules to accomplish the goals. Planning always has a purpose. I am often asking participants what goals or challenges have they set for themselves? What do you want to achieve in life? What do you want the end result to be? What contingency plans do you have in place? What and where are the potholes, hazards and challenges?

What are the priorities and risks? What will you see, smell, hear or feel? What will it look and sound like when you have achieved or are achieving your goals? How do you prepare for success? As the saying goes, 'Success hadn't come yet, so I went ahead without it'. Planning is also seen as a fore thought. It involves the process of thinking about and organising the activities required to achieve a desired goal. Planning includes the creation and maintenance of a plan. Make and work on your plan. It may be necessary to look at your surroundings and make changes, so that your goal(s) works for you rather than against you.

I often ask participants where they see themselves in a year's time, two (2) or five (5) years' time. Many respondents struggle to answer this question. They often reply that they can't even think about tomorrow, much less to think about 1-5 years. The key word here is to think; an activity of the brain which some people do not like to do. So instead of thinking of a plan, they think of not making plans or putting things off. That's much easier and less taxing on the brain; basically, doing nothing. My question is: 'Where does nothing get us?' The answer: 'Nowhere'. Remember, you have go ahead to get ahead.

What plans have you made, so that when adversity or the challenges of life or work comes, you can deal with them? You have to plan differently. You have to build in the good times so that when problems come, you are prepared. What is your Plan A and where is your Plan B? What contingencies do you have in place? I live my life asking **'what if'** questions rather than having **'if only'** thoughts. Over the years, I have worked with managers and staff who have undergone re-structuring, been made redundant or were retiring from their organisations. The discussions have centred on dealing with the unknown and how prepared are individuals regarding their futures.

Being prepared means you need to be informed. Two of my favourite quotes are: 'If you think education is costly, then try ignorance' and 'Ignorance is not bliss'. We need to be better informed or aware at least, so that we can plan and make better choices and decisions regarding our lives and futures.

From personal experiences, I have paid dearly for making poor choices and decisions because I did not have all the facts or information. Are we operating in a state of ignorance? Where do you source or get information from? Who do you speak or listen to? The people that you talk to or take advice from; what is their lifestyle like? It is said that great minds discuss ideas, average minds discuss events and small minds discuss people. Another take on the quote is 'wealthy people talk about ideas whereas poor people talk about money'. Where are you? One of my favourite questions is: Whose wing are you under? Who has your ears? Who are your role models? Who are your influencers?

We live in a social media fuelled age of selfies, body shaming and trolling which is having an adverse impact on the mental health and well-being of people of all ages and stages, particularly young people. A number of people live their entire lives through social media, being judged on social media, 'fake' news, 'twitter spats' and 'leaks' dominating the headlines. We are spending too much time idolising the outside of people which leads to contamination on the inside. We are getting 'social media' depression. Are you worried about your 'likes'; who 'likes' you or who doesn't 'like' you? We want people to like us and we don't even like, much less love ourselves. How can that be?

Social media and the internet are constant and everywhere and there is an onslaught of information and misinformation. We have so much information but so little knowledge. We need to question everything now, more than ever before. How easy is it to spot fake news? Where do the leaks come from? Have you been caught out in terms of fake news? Is the information accurate or correct? Is it believable? Who or what are your sources? Can they be trusted? I love this quote – 'Trust me I am a doctor'. 'A Spin doctor'. Don't compare yourself on social media. A lot of it is not real. It's fake. I believe that we need to learn a new skill of navigating the world of news today. Changing the people you listen to will alter the way that you see the world. We need to do a reality check on the sharing of information and think twice before we share. These are my thoughts on the sharing of information.

'Before sharing information, check its source, is it correct, accurate, true and sent in love? Most importantly does it enhance yours and other people's well-being?'

Vision - 'I Have A Dream'

Planning requires visioning – having a vision. Are you prudent or paranoid? Do you have a dream? Are you a person of purpose and/or destiny? Do you have a vision? Do you consider yourself to be a 'visionary' or 'vision caster'? I am often reminded of the iconic Dr. Martin Luther King Jr. delivering what is commonly known as the 'I have a dream' speech. Vision is a seeing word. How's your vision, 20/20? Are you long sighted or short sighted? Do you need glasses, contact lenses or laser eye surgery to see clearer? Do you realise that sight without vision is worse than blindness? Is it more insight and less eyesight that is needed? Open your vision.

What is vision? It is a clear and mental image/picture of what the future will be or could be like. It involves the ability to think about or plan the future with imagination and/or wisdom. It is the ability to see something. The picture is internal and personal. Vision provides direction. It brings the future into focus. It is a focal point of reference. Vision grabs hold and won't let go. You think big when you have a vision. What is your vision of the future? A song comes to mind, 'I can see clearly now the rain is gone, I can see all obstacles in my way. . .' What do you see regarding your life and your future?

Visualisation is sustaining a mental picture of what you want from life. A picture really does paint a thousand words. Remember the old adage: Without the vision, the people perish, without the people the vision perishes. Do you have a sound and compelling vision? Define your vision. When you have vision you control where you are going. Vision creates a sense of purpose and is a vital first step to ensuring the motivation and achievement of goals. Make a statement. Don't be confined or defined by anybody. Hold and check your vision and don't give up on it.

Communicate the vision with simplicity and clarity. Another of my favourite words is 'simplicity'. I believe in a simple life. I love things that are easy and straight forward. Do you know anyone who wants a complicated life? I am always encouraging participants to write 'Vision/Mission Statements' about their future. See, speak and run with the vision. Use every opportunity and medium to spread the word.

'Never lose sight of your vision!'

We lose our vision because we focus on our condition. Just focus on your vision and you will do things that are humanly incomparable. Most importantly, don't let people who have no vision, vote on yours. Realising your vision is your goal. You need to live the vision by taking action that brings results. It's time to map out your destination.

'The only way to predict your future is to create it!'

Goal Setting

Goals . . . Goals . . and more Goals! (We are not talking football!)

- What goals have you set yourself?

- What personal targets have you set yourself?

- What are your short, medium and long term goals?

- What do you want to achieve?

- What are your priorities?

- Are you fulfilling your own prophecy?

- What persistent dreams or re-occurring ideas do you have?

- What are your life ambitions?

- How are you going to achieve them?

What is a goal?

Part of planning is goal setting. Another question that I often ask participants is: 'In the next six (6) to twelve (12) months, what is the one goal that you would have achieved, that would be the biggest impact on your life? For some people, the word 'goal(s)' can be so challenging and overbearing that it prevents people from starting or thinking about it. So, it may be helpful to think of goals as a '**To Do List with Deadlines**' or '**steps**' to be taken to achieve a desired end result. In my case, I call it a '**Must Do**' list.

Goals may also be referred to as 'aims', 'objectives', 'targets', 'outcomes' or 'results'. What is important is that you have them on both a personal and professional basis and you know how to identify them correctly. Goals can also be described as 'action plans' because they specify what you intend to do in the future. They represent a commitment to action. According to Brian Tracey, 'People with goals move ahead, people without goals work with people with goals'. Put another way, if you don't know where you are going, you follow or go with others. You need to be clear about your goals, know what your vision is, communicate that vision or goal to others and get them involved. Make sure you have got people around you and get them to buy into your goals/ambition. Goals are things that you can make happen. Choose your goals carefully.

Why Goals?

Goal setting techniques are used by individuals from a variety of fields. They give you long-term vision and short-term motivation. In terms of planning and organising ourselves, goals give us something to work towards, to achieve. In terms of setting personal and professional goals they help you to organise your time, resources and most importantly your life.

The setting of goals is important in helping you to know and choose where you want to go in life. By knowing exactly what you want to achieve, you will know where you have to concentrate your thoughts and efforts and avoid distractions. Your goals will need to be clear if you are to manage your time effectively and efficiently. They need to be firmly established in your mind. Your overall goal(s) can be broken down into sub-goals. It's about you taking charge of your life and creating your own future, starting now. Goal setting is about making your vision a reality and bridging the gap between where you are now and where you want to be.

As far as I am concerned life is always a deadline. Give yourself some deadlines to work towards. Meaningful vision and realistic goals must include; an explanation of the goal and a date for completion. However, don't spend your thoughts and time on 'Some Day Isle', as your goals need to contain appropriate information and they must be carefully set and agreed upon.

They should be guided by the following principles.

SMARTER Goals

'Start setting SMARTER Goals for yourself"

Specific	• Be precise with what you want to achieve • They should not be vague or abstract, use action words/verbs
Measurable	• Measure the cost, quality, quantity and time • You need to be able to measure your goals – decide on how you are going to measure your goals
Achievable/ Attainable	• Will you be able to achieve the goals set and agreed upon? • Make sure that all the people who need to be involved agree.
Realistic	• Can you achieve the task agreed upon? • Is it practical?
Timely	• Set deadlines, so that you know your expectations • Include milestones and completion date(s)
Energy/ Environment	• Consider the amount of energy it takes as well as the environment you are in, to accomplish the goal
Record	• Put goals in writing

- List all possible steps

- Establish the things that are most important to you and arrange these in order of priority

- Keep the statements about your goals - Short and Simple (**K.I.S.S**)

- State your goals in the positive

- Generate a list of problems or opportunities

- Identify possible requirements

- Develop goals for solutions

- Generate possible solutions

- Develop action plans

- Determine your success criteria (evidence of successful completion) – How will you know that your goal has been achieved?

- Always ask 'What if' questions.

- Think about how you will negotiate your goals

Goals can be added to, subtracted from and most importantly taken off your list - as you go through life. Every season in life asks you a different set of questions. There is the need to focus on the completion of one goal at a time and then move on to the next. Never give up on your goals just because of the time it will take to achieve them. Remember, the time will pass anyway. In terms of goals, always think of how far you have come and not how far you have got to go. Tell yourself that you can see the invisible and do the impossible.

Take action on your goals. Where there's a will, there's a way or as I sometimes say, where there's no will there's no way. A goal with no action is going nowhere. No action, no movement. If you keep on driving and looking in the rear-view mirror, you will have an accident. You cannot waste your time living in the last chapter of your life. Stop looking back in your history and staying there. All you can do is re-play the past, play to the present and pre-play the future. The key to your development and achievement is the optimum utilisation of your skills, abilities, knowledge, experiences and strengths.

Spidergram/Patterned Notes

One way of identifying as well as recording your goal(s) is through the Spidergram (Spider diagram)/Patterned Note Taking technique. Organise your thinking using Spidergrams and create powerful thought patterns to bring your goal/vision to life. It is about putting your goal into focus and improving the quality of your thinking. It can be creative and self expressive. It is about focusing on what is important to you in terms of your goal(s) and success. A Spidergram can help outline key aspects of your goals. Helping you to shape your future and make the right decisions.

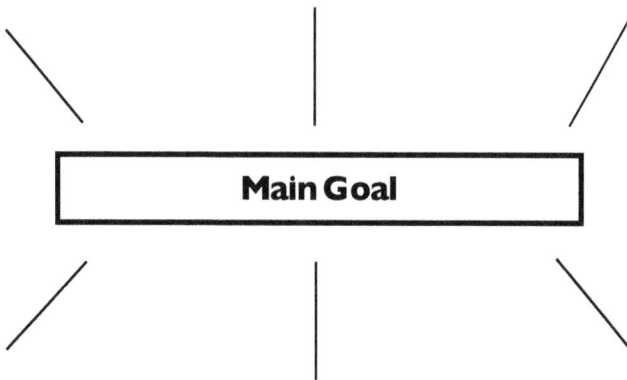

```
  \           |           /
   \          |          /
    \         |         /
 ┌─────────────────────────┐
 │        Main Goal        │
 └─────────────────────────┘
    /         |         \
   /          |          \
  /           |           \
```

How are Spidergrams/Patterned notes done?

- Take a sheet of paper and write your main or overarching goal in the middle

- Draw lines (known as hierarchical line, with nodes coming off them)

- Write down sub goals or key words/phrases/sentences/ideas in terms of your goals, starting from the centre or corners and branching off, indicating connecting points

- Establish priority areas, indicating connecting points

- Indicate key choices, decisions and actions required

- Generate as many ideas as possible about your goals

The following questions are intended to help you think through and identify or solidify your goals via the Spidergram technique.

- What is your one clear goal for the future?

- What risks are you prepared to take?

- What will make your heart sing?

- What do you love to do?

- What bold innovative step are you going to take?

- How daring are you going to be?

- What is the big picture?

- Do you trust your instincts?

- What are your instincts telling you to do in relation to your goals?

- How adventurous are you in your thinking and planning?

- Is it feasible?

- Is it right for you?

- What are your own set of rules for what you want to do/are doing?

- What requirements do you need for the future?

- What options are available to you?

Reviewing your goals – the key to success

You need to take time out and review your goals and plans, to see if you are on track. This will require the following:

- Review the last six (6) months or the past year to see how you have done and what you can change or improve.

- Evaluate your current position. Do an objective review of what you are achieving now. Which goals are you meeting or not meeting? Did you achieve your goals? If yes, what evidence do you have that supports this? If not, why not?

- Do a quick review on a monthly/weekly basis. Ask yourself if the goals set are still important to you? You may need to re-prioritise your goals, time and activities to make them happen.

- You may also need to build and review your contingency plans.

Attitude and Values

What's your attitude to life, people and success? What do you value? What are your values?

Think positively as you begin a new day, week, month, year. So that when negative situations stare you in the face, you will be able to cope. Attitude is everything. Choose your attitude, choose your life. Your attitude determines your success and access. You need to develop a winning attitude, a way of thinking that gives you total confidence that you will achieve your goals. One of my key phrases is 'Say it like you mean it'. Your attitude and skills equal success in life. If you believe it, you will achieve it.

'Your attitude determines your success and access!'

Remember, never allow the attitude of someone to dictate or disturb your mood or state of mind. We teach people how to treat us. You are in control of your attitude and based on how you deal with a situation, it determines whether you are a master of your emotion as against it being a master of you. You need to let go of the **'Dinosaur mentality'** – particularly in how you view and see life and deal with challenging situations.

What are your expectations of life? As for me; I expect, so I get. I am always expecting things to happen or to have a positive outcome. As far as I am concerned the glass is overflowing and not half full or half empty. Your view will depend partly on your expectations. The reality of things/ life will change in your mind according to these expectations. Change one and the other will change too.

We tend to look at life according to our values. What's your value base? If you believe in personal wealth, you may see those who have acquired fortunes as people who are to be admired or on the other hand, you may see them as greedy. However you view them, they will have the same amount of money either way, but your values will cause you to see them differently. I love this saying: 'You realise you don't have money until you meet someone who has'. There isn't anything more to be said there.

Time - Tick Tock, Beat the Clock!

'Seconds are too fast - Hours are too few - Days are too busy'

One of the areas that we overlook or underestimate is time. Time – we all have been given the same amount, but we never seem to have enough. Time is fixed. There is only twenty four (24) hours in a day, it is not more or less. (How I wish.) Have you ever said or heard the following sayings: 'I haven't got the time', 'I am running out of time', 'I need more time', or 'where did the time go?' As my mother would always say: 'Time is money - you can either invest in it or lose it'. Another of my mother's sayings about time is: 'You cannot manage time, time will manage you.' I am intrigued by the following paradox. Why is it that we don't have more time with all the technology we've added to our lives? It's simple. We keep adding more information and activities to our lives. Our expectation for productivity has increased and we are exhausted and stressed with the pace of our lives.

It's Question Time!

- What does time mean to you?

- How do you manage time?

- How are your time management skills?

- What goals/targets/outcomes are you required to meet?

- How do you set them?

- What things take up your time?

- What are your priorities and deadlines?

- How do you prioritise your workload?

- How do you meet your deadlines?

- How do you spend your time?

- What do you do with your time? Do you edify, educate or entertain yourself?

- How do you deal with other people's time, agendas, priorities and deadlines?

- What aids/tools do you use to plan your day/week?

- Do you need to save time?

- Who are you giving your time to?

- What are the main barriers to you using your time well?

- How can you eliminate these?

What is Time Management?

Time management is wisely using one of your most precious resources - **TIME** - to achieve your key goals. It means investing time to make time. *Time management is life management*. Time management is managing yourself in relation to time and the activities/tasks you need to do. How you manage your time, dictates how you manage your life. Time management is a set of principles, structures and a series of tools and techniques used to manage time when accomplishing specific tasks, projects and goals. They are to help you increase your efficiency and productivity, so that you get more value out of your time with the aim of improving the quality of your life. Time management is working smarter not harder. You need to make time management a lifestyle of effective habits which create balance in your life.

As the saying goes: 'Time flies when you are having fun, or it drags when you are not'. Basically, time waits on no one. As my mother would often say: 'Time is not going to stop for you.' 'Neither is the train nor the plane going to wait on you'. Unfortunately, you cannot freeze time. Time management is about reviewing how you spend your time so you can determine what changes you need to make to become more productive in work and life generally.

'Tomorrow is the most dangerous word!'

Managing your time effectively requires certain processes and approaches. It involves knowing, understanding and using a variety of tools and techniques - whether technology or pen and paper. The key time management techniques require changing the way you think – mind-sets, attitudes, behaviour, bad habits and how tasks are undertaken, which for some isn't easy and will take time. It is examining ways to maximise your performance output in terms of your time. It is about taking personal responsibility and control for managing time, work and life more successfully. It's about breaking poor time management habits and learning new or better ones. Most importantly, it is creating work/life balance. When you use your time wisely, you become more focused.

Time Management Approaches:

A number of time management approaches have been discussed throughout the book and include the following:

- Effective planning

- Setting goals, targets, outcomes and objectives

- Planning when and how to achieve your goals

- When are you at your best? Be aware of times during the day when you're at your best – plan your most demanding work, projects and activities for these times.

- Identify where you are currently spending your time – and what's getting in the way of achieving your goals

- Improve your efficiency

- Learn to read 'smarter'

- Think and question, then prioritise

- Prioritise your work/tasks – what needs to be done first?

- Be organised – use different systems/programmes/'Apps'/ computerised/electronic diaries

- Set agendas for the day/week

- Set time limits for getting tasks done and stick to it

- Make changes in the way you work or undertake tasks

- If you don't complete a task, don't stress – just re-assess!

- Be a starter and a finisher

- Review your progress and evaluate impact of the changes

- Start the process again; review time usage against your goals and objectives

- Avoid panic, stress and worry; they are time wasters. Keep a clearly focused mind

- Get into effective time keeping habits

- Set yourself some time rules and live by them

- Don't procrastinate! Don't delay - Do It Now! Just Do It!

- Look at how you deal with paperwork/correspondence, phone calls, the dreaded 'emails' and social media in general – what do you need to change or do differently?

- Be gracious with people and ruthless with paper/correspondence

- Stop the time wasters! Look at how you deal with distractions, interruptions, visitors and meetings – what do you need to change or do differently?

- Ask for help – there are some things that you cannot do on your own!

These Tools and Techniques Will Work *If* You Work With Them.

Your time is up!

Mirror Check:

Time Management

I love the 'Three (3) D' and the '123' Approaches:

'Three D' Approach:

- Do
- Delegate
- Dump/Discontinue

Rate each task on importance using the **'123'** scale:

1 = Unimportant - Would not result in major problems if not done

2 = Important - Would cause serious problems if not done

3 = High - Must be finished

Then rate each task on urgency using the **'123'** scale:

1 = Low - Can be done anytime

2 = Medium - Must be done within the next week/few weeks

3 = High - Must be finished today/this week

Author's Reflection

I love these time management reflections:

I can only please one person each day. Today is not your day. Tomorrow does look too good either.

Not meeting your deadline, does not make it mine.

Did you know that how many 'got a minute?' Takes minutes.

Nothing makes a person more productive than the last minute.

If you don't have time to do it right, you must have time to do it over.

Time heals almost everything, give it time.

You can't save time, you can only invest it.

Time is not an equation for success

There's no time like the present.

Make time work for you!

Mirror Challenge 'Respond' Exercise:

Time Management 'Action Plan':

What are the main barriers to you using your time well?	
How can you eliminate these?	
How can you improve your efficiency?	
What can you do right now to manage your time more effectively?	

How did you find doing this exercise?

Mirror Challenge
'Respond' Exercise:

Challenge Yourself

What is the key thing that you want to see happen in your lifetime?

What small step could you take towards that purpose today?

How did you find doing this exercise?

*Mirror Challenge
'Respond' Exercise:*

Challenge Yourself

Make a list of things that you would like to achieve in life. (The list is based on your next significant birthday, i.e. if you are going to be 20, 30, 40 or 50 years old, then your list should have 20, 30, 40 or 50 items/activities!)

How did you find doing this exercise?

Mirror Challenge 'Respond' Exercise:

In terms of taking action:

Change (What do you need to change?)	Stop (What do you need to stop doing?)	Start (What do you need to start doing?)	Different (What do you need to do differently?)

How did you find doing this exercise?

Mirror Challenge 'Respond' Exercise:

The MIRROR Plan

What are your plans/goals for the future?

It's time to get started on the plan. Give yourself some quiet time, put on some relaxing music and open your mind to all possibilities. Don't even think about restricting yourself. To help you with this process, re-visit a number of questions that have been asked in earlier chapters of this book.

How did you find doing this exercise?

Mirror Challenge
'Respond' Exercise:

Vision and More Vision

'I can see clearly . . .'

What is your vision for the future?

Write three (3) Vision/Mission Statements about your future.

●

●

●

How can you make the vision a reality?

How did you find doing this exercise?

Mirror Challenge 'Respond' Exercise:

Goals, Goals and More Goals!

What are your goals for the next three (3) months (bearing in mind the SMARTER Goals guidelines)?

How did you find doing this exercise?

Mirror Challenge
'Respond' Exercise:

Goals and sub-goals

(a) Write down one main, overall goal for yourself:

(b) Now split this goal into at least three sub-goals:

(i)

(ii)

(iii)

How did you find doing this exercise?

Mirror Challenge
'Respond' Exercise:

Goals and Spidergrams

Complete a Spidergram of one of your goals.

How did you find doing this exercise?

Mirror Challenge 'Respond' Exercise:

Reflection and Review Exercise and Action Planning

Discovery	Reflection
What have I learnt about myself? What have I learnt that is new or different?	What have been the main learning points or lessons for me?
Changes	**Action**
What needs to change? Is it my attitude, language or behaviour? How I approach my work? How I relate to others?	What are the Priority Areas for actioning? What action do I need to take or do to achieve these changes/goals?
Resources/Support	**Review/Targeted Times**
What resources or support is needed? What is needed to achieve these goals or changes as described above?	What timescales am I working towards? When do I want to achieve these goals?

Mirror Challenge 'Respond' Exercise:

Action Planning:

Action Point	How will the action be carried out?	Completion Date	Outcome

How did you find doing this exercise?

Author's Reflection

I was on holidays and visited a well-known Department store. A massive sale was taking place and people were buying as if there was no tomorrow. (Well who said 'tomorrow' is guaranteed?) At the end of shopping, we had to join a very long queue to pay for the goods. I observed that there were two and at one time only one cashier serving this very long queue of customers. I just couldn't fathom that out. We were in the queue for a very long time and people's patience and tempers had begun to fray.

One woman had the boldness and started vocalising how we all were feeling in terms of this long wait to get to a cashier. A supervisor/cashier heard her complaining about the poor customer service and how the store/management had been treating its customers. The cashier came over to placate the customer and to apologise for the long wait. What followed next is classic. The woman said to the cashier: "Your apology is not helping the situation, you have left your cash register and I am on a lunch break and all we need you to do is get more cashiers, so that we can pay for our things and leave your store!" This was said to a rapturous applause. Within minutes, another two cashiers 'appeared' from somewhere and the line began to move a whole lot faster.

What came into my spirit was that: 'Words are not enough' and the song: 'Sorry does not always make it right' is not right at this moment. People want and expect more/better. For most of the times, people don't want words or platitudes – because a lot of it can be meaningless. They want action! They want something done/somebody to do something. Any action, real action and with real people (not a machine) taking action/doing their jobs. Doing something. People have needs and they need to be met or solved as quickly as is humanly possible.

Remember, actions speak louder than words!

Mirror Check:

Consider the Following:

- **What Can You Control? . . . . You, Not Others**

- **What Can You Do Now? . . . . Think Strengths and Positives**

- **What Do You Want To Do? . . . . Focus Your Thinking**

- **What Do We Need To Do? . . . . Prioritise and Focus Your Energy Now**

Author's Reflection

I love the following affirmations:

- 'The happiest of people don't necessarily have the best of everything; they just make the most of everything they have'.

- 'Life may not be the party we hoped for, but while we are here we might as well dance'.

Remember:

There are Four Kinds of People in the world:

1. Those who do not have a clue as to what is happening

2. Those who wait for things to happen

3. Those who watch things happen

4. Those who make things happen!!

Which one are you?

Make sure you are one of those people who make things happen for you!

Have a Mirror Moment!

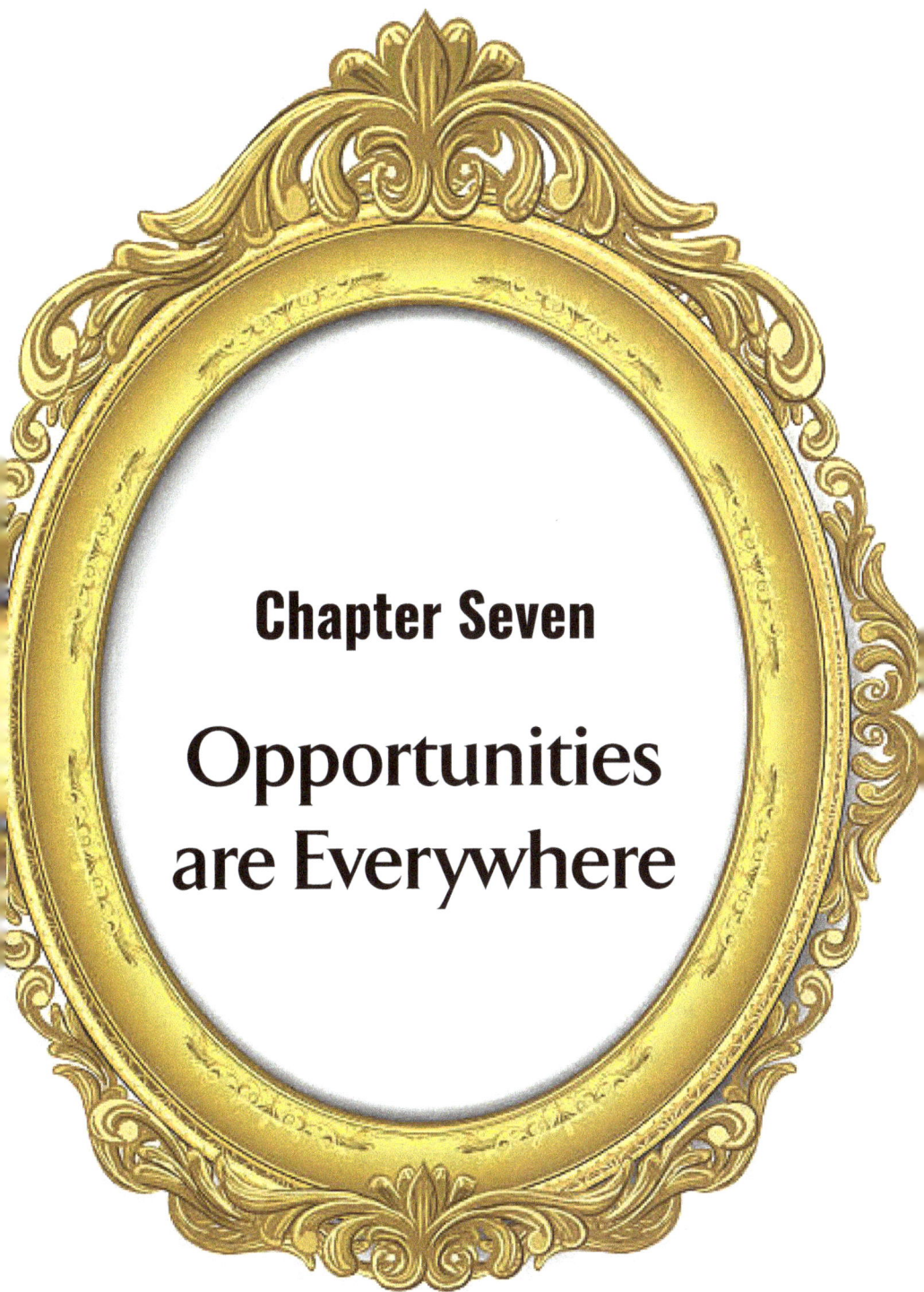

Chapter Seven

Opportunities are Everywhere

When problem solving, a favourite question of mine to participants is: 'Do you have the means, motive or opportunity?' Likewise, another of my sayings on training is: 'Opportunities are everywhere, but if you are not looking, you don't see them'. My parents would often say: 'There is no generation that has more opportunities than this one'. I view opportunities as possibilities. As the saying goes: Life is full of possibilities. In business they are seen as 'leads'. A favourite and a very interesting acronym is '**POOR**', which explains brilliantly why some people are in the state that they are in!

Passing

Over

Opportunities

Repeatedly

Where are the opportunities?

What and where are the possibilities? As the saying goes they are endless. The sky is not the limit, just the view. Opportunities can occur as a result of change, chaos, contention, disillusion, challenges, confusion, frustration, dissatisfaction, inconsistencies, ambiguity, difficulties, insecurity and uncertainty, to name a few. Every opportunity has a shelf life, so make the most of them. Focus on what you can do and not what you can't do. As they say in football: It's not just creating chances but taking them that counts. The MIRROR Challenge wants you to look, find and take action regarding these areas of opportunity, if you want to advance or progress to the next level or move on in life.

Remember, there is no such thing as a crisis, but an opportunity. Create opportunities. See, seize and discover opportunities (they may be coming from a distance!) Don't wait for opportunities. They are staring you in the mirror. They are in your face. Mistakes are an opportunity for you to grow. If you have failed and made mistakes that make it seem impossible for you to succeed, then the key is to persevere. Never stop seeking opportunities for growth and development. Prepare yourself for opportunities. Be open to opportunity and not scrutiny. Moments don't last a lifetime, there are only some moments. Remember, doors do not remain open for long, so walk through and step out. I keep on hearing the following comments, when I have challenged someone to do something – 'I am too small', 'I am too thin', 'I am too fat',' 'I am too old', 'I am too young', 'I am too busy', 'I am too tired', 'I am too late'. "It's too much' or 'tomorrow'. My reply usually is 'why not too-day?'

Life is unpredictable and opportunities are all about dealing with the unexpected and the need to be spontaneous. My high school motto was: 'Carpe Diem' – 'seize the day'. Opportunities are about seizing the moment; doing it now. I am aware that I do not have time to wait for things that need to be done. I realise that you can do better to make things better. It's about inspiring confidence in yourself and your abilities as well as in others. You cannot seize an opportunity that you cannot see. So, start seeing it in your mind, your vision. Picture it. Another favourite saying of mine is: 'See yourself in the future'. Start claiming things before you even have them. You never know when an opportunity may come your way. Is your lifelong hobby to do something that you haven't done before? Remember that you can't live in freedom, if you keep on doing what you always done. It is said that a flashback is the opportunity to a comeback as well as a setback is the opportunity to a comeback. Be ready! On your marks, get set and go!

Looking in the Mirror, Questions to ask Yourself:

● What choices are available to you?

● What are the choices for you to grow and develop?

● What are the opportunities for you to grow and develop?

● Where are the opportunities for you to grow and develop?

- Who do you need to help or support you along the way?

- What resources or things will you need?

- Are you creating your own opportunities?

- Have you created your own opportunities?

- How ready are you in dealing with challenging situations?

'New Opportunities, New Challenges!'

We must always remember that with opportunities come challenges and opposition and we must be prepared for them. What are your challenges? What are your limits, parameters, boundaries and conditions?

The Ladder of Opportunity

Mirror Challenge 'Opportunity' Exercise:

Opportunities – What opportunities are available to you now?

What are the things that you could do or take action on that would help you to develop or reach your potential?

What do you want to do?

How did you find doing this exercise?

Change – 'The Reality Check'

'Change happens, so shift!'

A key aspect in terms of opportunity is change. To some people – 'change' is the dreaded word. What words would you use to describe change? What do you feel when you think about change? What and who can you change? The answer is **You** and no one else. Only you can change you. One of the biggest changes that you need to make is in and on yourself. We need to be changed and challenged. You be the change. As I regularly say: 'I don't do change, I am the change'.

'Change is hard, but NOT impossible.'

Change is a choice. Life is about change. A nurse asked a patient if he was allergic to anything. He replied: 'life!' He needed a seismic change on how he viewed himself and life in general. Are you allergic to change? Are you a wall or a bridge to your destiny? Let's be real, change is necessary. As far as I am concerned, patience maybe a virtue but sheer obstinacy is not. Change has become a way of life for most of us. Ever travelled on the underground and heard the announcer say: 'All change, all change please.' They are talking about you. The hardest thing in life is for people to change. People will do everything else in life but change. We cannot force people to change who they are and the situations they are in.

A number of people think that if their wives, husbands, partners, colleagues and friends changed then their life would be better or different. In reality, it's you that needs to change and not them. You cannot change anyone but yourself. People have got to want to change for themselves. They have got to want and feel the need to change or it will not happen. You need to be flexible and adaptable to change.

If you change the way you act you will alter the way that people respond to you. It will also affect the things that you do and in turn the things that you encounter. Overtime, your change will eventually impact others. The ripple effect - once you have changed, you will notice that others have changed as well.

When it comes to making our lives really worth living, there are two options: Change or wonder what might have been. Don't be haunted by the ghost of your past and/or 'what ifs' in your life. Choose change. It may not come overnight but it will come. I have learnt that there is a real power in managing change. In the 'meantime', while waiting, look for elements in life, business and situations that you can control. We need to focus on the small things for the big/drastic change to happen. We have got to start again – gut the house and re-build it from the foundation up. It starts with telling the world who you really are. Real change begins from the inside out and not the outside in.

CHANGED PRIORITIES AHEAD

'Only You can change You!'

Author's Reflection

On a Self-Development/Self Marketing course, participants were asked to complete a Personal Statement. The honesty of the individuals was so powerful and profound. One participant commented on her age and that she was not doing very much with her life apart from getting up-going to work, coming home, and going to bed. The group laughed but the reality was that this was the daily routine of a number of people. When asked: 'Where are you now and what do you want to do?' The participant replied: 'In a home and a job that I do not want to be in.' She added that she really wanted to move home, get a different job and go on holiday.

The discussions then centred on how participants were going to make that move. Most participants acknowledged that they were looking forward to the future bringing better things. In order for this to happen, some participants indicated that they needed to change direction completely while others agreed that they needed to watch out for opportunities to move on. They all recognised that they needed to take action, not just say it, but do something, do something different or they would continue to be a 'getting up, going to work, coming home and going to bed' person'.

Another participant actually commented: 'I woke up and realised that there must be more to life, started to commit myself to a career and enjoying life.' Another individual said that they expected that things would come with their own effort.

'The power to change'

Inspired 2 Change

The MIRROR Challenge is about the power to change. The change begins with you. It starts with you. It's time to make positive changes. I am always telling participants that if they don't like something; change it. If you change nothing, nothing will change. You are a product of what you do habitually. You might simply choose to look at your habits. We need to get rid of some bad habits and acquire new ones. We use to be told that it takes 21 days for a habit to be formed, but the new thinking is that it takes 100 days for a habit to become a lifetime. If you want your life to change, it has to start with what you think (mind), say (mouth); that will ultimately lead to your actions. The quality of your choices determines the quality of your life. There are certain things you've got to stop saying if you're ever going to break through your mental barriers and self-imposed limitations. If you do different things the world will be subtly different. It's time to break the mould. Remember, it is only the foolish that believes that the same behaviour gets you a different result. Also remember: 'I did then what I knew how, now I know better I do better.' What are the changes that you need to make? What and where are the options and alternatives? Once you make a decision, just follow through.

It is said that: 'A smart person knows their limits but a wise person knows they have none.' Only you can control how you think and act and no one else. Build another picture of you. You need to re-position, re-set, re-programme your thinking, expectations, beliefs, attitude, values and ideologies. You need new ways of working, decision making and problem solving. Most importantly, you need to change your mind-set, language and have a new way of speaking and dealing with the challenges of life. You need to change your conditional response patterns and false belief systems. Take control over your mind, what and how you say things. Change what you think is possible. Empower your thought processes. Your situation is not defining you, it's re-defining you.

Mirror Check:

Consider the Following:

- **Refocusing**
- **Recreating**
- **Restarting**
- **Revamping**
- **Remodelling**
- **Rethinking**
- **Renewing**
- **Rebuilding**
- **Redoing**
- **Rejuvenating**
- **Refreshing**
- **Reworking**
- **YOU!**

'If you change nothing, nothing will change!'

We need to get away from those who are framing our thinking. I personally divorce myself from the opinions of people that are harmful and unproductive. This is where people have to learn to let go of the old and take on the new. Although change is a constant factor of life, it can be difficult to deal with and accept. In order to survive the complexities of life, you will need the flexibility to master the most personal and professional challenges/changes. Change offers both uncertainty and opportunity and how you manage that change will make all the difference. There will be the need to continually accomplish changing goals.

Your goal is to turn change into an opportunity. In order for you to explore the opportunities, the mirror needs you to change, make adjustments. Take a step back and make those changes. Be prepared to try new things. Do something different. Take a calculated risk. Challenge yourself. It could be time for a new or fresh start. Your desire changes your destiny. Only you can make a difference. You have to wake up each day and renew your commitments to yourself. It only takes a moment to change your life/future. It's funny, our lives can turn on a single moment's decision. One decision has the power to change everything. Remember one small change makes a big difference. A small detail can lead to a big result. Small keys open big doors and small hinges hang on big doors. Make this your season for change. The time to change is now. Remember, the tables turned, because you turned. Are you making change real for yourself? Mahatma Gandhi has reminded us that: 'We have to become the change we want to see.'

Change the Story - What needs to change?

The MIRROR wants you to change your:

- Thinking
- Expectations
- Profile

- Choices
- Decisions
- Attitude
- Values
- Language
- Habits
- Actions
- Behaviour
- Ways of working/doing things

'To change your outside, change your inside first.'

There is the need for you to upgrade yourself. We upgrade our phones, computers, tablets and gadgets but not ourselves. We put security on our phones, but not on our hearts, minds, souls and lives. You need to change your password. Everything is changing except us. You can change anything you want. What's your capacity? Has it expanded? Put yourself out there. Success comes with getting that break. What do you want to break today? Change is forcing you out of your comfort zone. Change your situation and pursue your dreams. Technology is changing the way we do things, how we work and our lives. The rules and even games are changing.

Why not imagine your life in a completely different way? Look at things differently. Go for things that you want and not what society tells you, you should do. I am always reminding participants not to worry about the after effects, but more about the effects. I have learnt to accept change and not to defy it, as it can destroy you. Change is inevitable, so it is better to engage change rather than defend against it. Don't just play the game.

Change it. Most importantly, I have also learnt that change does not need my permission, change happens and if you are not careful, you are left behind. So, shift! Move!

'Become your own change agent and the architect of your future.'

In terms of change, consider the following:

● Establish trust as a cornerstone

● Become an agent of preparation

● Become an agent of options and solutions

● Become an agent of closure

● Become an agent of change

● Be an architect of the future

● Be a self-educator

● Be aware of being obsolete and keep up dated

● Some knowledge has a shelf life – embrace continuous learning, development and improvement

● Understand current challenges and avoid being pigeon-holed

● Tap into the unconventional wisdom that abounds in your network, sphere as well as yourself

Mirror Check:

Remember:

- Life changes and so should you.
- There are many ways to change the world; find yours.
- Nothing changes if you don't let it.
- When we change, the world changes too.
- If you don't like the direction your life is taking – Change It.
- Put all of your strength and determination into making a positive change in your life.

Author's Reflection

I recently watched a documentary where the main person in the story indicated that 'something' needed to change, but was not acknowledging that it had anything to do with them.

However, the documentary was clearly indicating that they needed to change - their attitude and behaviour as a starter.

Mirror Challenge Change Exercise:

Exercise: Change One Thing

What is the one thing you want to change?

How did you find doing this exercise?

Mirror Check:

When You Change Your. . . .

**When you change your thinking
You change your beliefs.**

**When you change your beliefs
You change your expectations.**

**When you change your expectations
You change your attitude.**

**When you change your attitude
You change your behaviour.**

**When you change your behaviour
You change your performance.**

**When you change your performance
You change your life!**

Author's Reflection

Laugh when you can

Apologise when you should

and let go of what you can't change.

'Get ready as your life is about to change!'

What is Continuing Personal Development (CPD)?

Another aspect of opportunity is personal or continuous development. This is known as CPD, which is the continuing development of yourself. It is the conscious updating of your personal knowledge, skills, competences and experience that you have gained either formally or informally. Improvement and growth are your ambition and aim. The word 'conscious' implies that CPD is a state of mind more than a set of rules or a programme of study. It is a process of recording and reflecting on your learning and development. It is your commitment to keep yourself up to date throughout your lifetime.

The process helps you to manage your own development on an ongoing basis. CPD starts with a period of personal reflection. Personal reflection is also discussed in some detail in Chapter Five of this book. It requires you taking time to ask yourself some key questions and noting the answers. The questions include the following:

- What have been your main achievements/highlights over the past year/two years?

- What are the most significant lessons that you have learnt?

- What are the factors that will influence you to undertake CPD?

The success of CPD ultimately depends on an ongoing willingness to learn and apply the lessons inherent in the experiences you have gained. It brings greater awareness of what you do, why you do it and how you do it. CPD can enhance your life prospects as well as be helpful in seeking lifetime opportunities. Ask yourself – are you fresh? Are you new? Do you know current thinking or practice in your field or area of work? Are you on an improvement journey?

'The KEY to life'

Keep Educating Yourself

Learning Log

As a trainer, one of the exercises that I undertake with participants is the development of a learning log. The learning log is a personal development tool that will assist you to reflect on and capture your thoughts and feelings in terms of what you have learnt or need to learn. One of the obvious questions is how do you learn? It is said that most things in life are not taught but caught.

There is no pre-set format for the log. It usually is a reflective piece of writing. It can take the form of dated entries, various pieces of writing or the drawing of pictures. It is up to you to devise a simple system of recording notes of your observations/learning. The log can help you to prepare an action plan to carry forward and you are better able to share your learning, growth and development with others. You may notice patterns of thought, behaviour or attitude. It is possible that you will also notice missed opportunities, errors of judgement or changes in levels of confidence. The log provides you with an opportunity to stand back and self-analyse your performance and experiences.

Learning Analysis - Questions to ask yourself:

The following questions will help you to focus on your learning:

- Where are you now?

- Where do you want to be?

- What do you have to do to get there?

- What do you need to learn and why?

- How do you learn?

- What are your strengths?

- What are your development areas?

- How can you capitalise on your strengths?

- How can you improve your development areas?

- What is driving you now?

- What new skill(s) do you need to learn/acquire and why?

- What new knowledge do you need to learn/acquire and why?

- Is it important for you to understand the theory behind what you are doing?

- What nuggets have you learnt?

- Are you a specialist or generalist in terms of your skills set?

- What are your sources of information?

- What are your sources and resources of learning?

- How do you expand your repertoire?

- What are the really important issues for you?

- Is your learning well planned?

- Do you like learning alone or with others?

- When do you review your progress?

- How will you review your progress?

- Do you review your experiences and consider what you have learnt?

- Can you locate any patterns or trends in terms of your behaviour or responses to specific situations?

- Can you recognise old patterns of thinking, behaviour and/or ways of working?

- Are there any newly recognised patterns?

No degree? No experience? No problem? So What?

Mirror Challenge 'Opportunity' Exercise:

Learning Log

Create your own Learning Log

How did you find doing this exercise?

Opportunities for Self Development

Investment in your Development

Are you aware of the seven (7) stages or '**ills**' of life?

1. Spills
2. Drills
3. Thrills
4. Bills
5. Ills
6. Pills
7. Wills

The question is what do you need to do? What do you need to change? The key to life is management and managing your time and change. How are you managing? Are you coping and not managing? Are you surviving and not thriving? Most importantly, how are *you* managing *you*? One of my favourite all time quotes is: *'If I were your life manager, I would sack you!'* You need to be developing both your professional and personal competences. We never graduate from life, we need to keep learning. A key question is how will you transfer and adapt your **S**kills, **A**bilities, **K**nowledge and **E**xperience (**SAKE**) to encompass change and open up new opportunities for you? There is the need to take time out and manage your own development. This will result in the unlocking of your potential and increase your confidence and competence. This involves reflecting critically on your practice/styles of working, how you manage and take personal responsibility for your own continuous professional development.

Self/Personal development is about meeting the growth and improvement needs of yourself - the skills, knowledge, attitudes and abilities needed for you to be effective and efficient. You need to realise that you have a responsibility to yourself and if you do not do it, nobody else will. As an individual you need to ensure that your own development is not side-lined or under prioritised. Are you one of those who has made a career limiting move or found yourself in such a situation? Have you stopped to study yourself? It is up to you to ensure that your skills remain up to date throughout your life. Commit yourself to continuously improving yourself and prioritising your own personal growth. We cannot graduate from life – we are perpetual students. Let's be real, you need to have some form of formal education or access to other forms of training in order to progress. In today's climate you need to refresh or update your knowledge on a regular basis to remain on top of your competence/game. It's your personality, your traits, your development, flexibility and being adaptable that will count in today's job market.

'Get your life back on track!'

Self/Personal Development – Questions to ask Yourself:

- What do you have to offer?
- What are your insights?
- What new ideas or goals do you have?
- What does any or all of that means for the future?
- Are you a practical person?
- Are you an intuitive person?
- Do you like to be well organised?
- Do you like working with others?
- Do you enjoy having a go?
- Do you like being shown how to do something?
- How flexible are you?
- Are you a morning, afternoon or evening person in terms of being productive?

- When are you at your best; morning, afternoon, evening or night?
- How well do you manage your time?
- Do you like asking questions?
- Do you admit when you are wrong or when you don't know?
- Do you learn from your mistakes?
- Do you learn from the mistakes of others?
- Do you listen?
- Do you listen to answers?
- Do you ask for help and advice when you need it?
- Are you a perfectionist or as long as the task is completed that's what matters?
- Do you recognise what you do well and how you do it?
- What tools and techniques do you need to manage your development?

Development Opportunities

Have you considered these as ways of developing yourself?

Work Based

- Learning by doing
- E-learning programmes
- On-line learning/training programmes
- Webinars
- Make the internet and social media work for you such as video and audio conferencing - Zoom, Skype, Microsoft Teams, LinkedIn, Twitter, Facebook, Instagram, YouTube, Mobile phone Applications – 'Apps' and blogs

- Case studies
- Reflective practice
- Clinical audit
- Attend lectures and training courses/programmes
- Attend conferences, seminars and talks
- Expand your work role
- Make a sideway move if necessary (it worked for me)
- Work shadowing
- Secondments
- Job rotation
- Supervising staff or students
- Network with individuals in roles you want to develop
- Join committees and working parties/groups
- Project work or project management
- Coaching from others
- Analysing significant events
- Discussions with colleagues
- Peer review
- Invite constructive feedback on your performance from colleagues and honest friends
- Member/involvement of a professional body/organisation
- Membership of a specialist interest group
- Gain a qualification

Non-Work Based

- E-learning programmes
- On-line learning/training programmes
- Webinars

- Make the internet and social media work for you such as video and audio conferencing - Zoom, Skype, Microsoft Teams, LinkedIn, Twitter, Facebook, Instagram, YouTube, Mobile phone Applications – 'Apps' and blogs - to gain information, learn and develop
- Set up a learning group – whether physically or online to exchange skills and knowledge amongst yourselves
- Carry out an audit on your successes and failures and learn from them
- Reflective practice
- Self–directed and informal learning
- Further education
- Develop new skills and acquire knowledge by attending a course or a course of study through a variety of platforms such as long distance learning - i.e the Open University
- Turn a hobby into a business/enterprise
- Market yourself
- Attend lectures and training courses/programmes
- Maintaining or developing specialist skills
- Network with individuals in roles you want to develop
- Read and research on a subject matter for information and ideas
- Listen to audios on the subject matter
- Watch educational programmes on a subject matter/areas of interest – a variety of platforms exist – television, social media, YouTube, computers, laptops, mobile phones, tablets – applications – 'Apps'
- Read relevant blogs, lifestyle magazines, specialist magazines, trade and professional magazines, journals, articles and books - to find out about trends
- Review books and articles
- Play games – word and card games and computer games
- Attend conferences, seminars, talks and social events

- Personal activities
- Observe a role model
- Keep a MIRROR diary/learning log of events and reflect on your learning experiences
- Join working parties, committees and meetings to gain experience
- Voluntary work - volunteer to take part in projects/activities that will stretch and develop you
- Ask to shadow someone who has the skills you want to develop
- Mentor someone who needs the skills you already have, it will be a learning experience for you both.
- Thinking/planning your contributions before speaking
- Always follow-up on any ideas and possibilities that relate to your personal and professional development
- Questionnaires – self assessment questionnaires, surveys and quizzes
- Get a qualification – it can make the difference
- Other

What are you seeking in terms of your development?

- Sense of identity and direction - knowing who you are and where you are going
- Appreciate who you are
- Lifelong learner and developer
- Effective communicator
- Continuous improvement and growth
- Enhancing performance
- Self-empowerment
- Working smarter, not harder
- Having a job/being in work

- New ways of working and learning
- Exploring varied and different options
- Rebuilding your future
- Self-employment/enterprise/business
- Employability through continuing development
- New skills, abilities, knowledge and competences
- Renewed confidence in yourself
- Choice in career paths and job roles
- The ability to plan for your financial security/future
- Choices in your work and life balance
- Information about the world of work and job opportunities/options
- Network of provision
- The ability to negotiate
- Problem solving

Author's Reflection

There is a joke that a man pondered a change of career, saying that he had more to give. However, one of his friends had this to say on the matter: 'Just because you haven't found your talent yet, it doesn't mean you have one.'

Another friend said: 'I knew he had it in him. It's just to find it that matters.'

(That's what I call an ouch!)

Personal and Professional Strategies for Growth and Development:

- Know Thyself! Know who you are first and remember it!
- Own your future – you owe it to yourself
- Broaden your horizon(s)
- Build your confidence – have a sense of who you are
- Develop your own mission, vision, values
- Look for opportunity in every situation
- Be ready for opportunity when it comes knocking
- Develop and keep an updated Curriculum Vitae (CV)
- Build a profile
- Create your vision
- Break bad habits

'Dare to be Different!'

- Don't procrastinate – it's the greatest thief of time. Destiny killer! It kills self-esteem and self- worth. Do it now!
- Start over or again.
- Start something - start your journey – who says it starts with money?
- Define what you want and ask for it.
- Focus, refocus and stay focus.
- Don't judge others, focus on yourself
- Think strategically rather operational – think and operate at a higher level.
- Know which battles you need to fight or are worth fighting – when did you win the battle but lost the war?

'Focus, refocus and stay focus'

- Do whatever is necessary to meet your goal.
- Stay in your lane – know your limit/roles/responsibilities – master your areas of work/interests.
- Look for opportunities for continuous improvement and growth.
- Pursue it, even if you don't have the experience or the money.
- Take advantage of networking contacts or build your own network and/or group. It is mooted that your key contact can be as close as three people away from you.
- We need more partners/alliances and not more borders.
- Don't make assumptions or feed into the stereotype.
- Don't ask for permission, ask for forgiveness.
- Be assertive in life and go after what you want. Do not let others tell you differently.
- Use the internet, websites and social media platforms to find information on how to . . .
- Strategically build your brand.
- Celebrate and learn from others.
- Copyright your work.
- Search for challenging opportunities to change, grow, innovate and improve.
- Make your own set of rules for what you want to do and stick to it.
- Let's be honest you need to look the part - appearance is paramount to success.
- Be real. Deal in reality. Think realistically.
- Increase your visibility, audibility and fluency.
- Nurture the perception of yourself as someone who can do/get things done or who has access to others who can get things done.

- Do the things that you really don't want to do first.
- Don't break the rules, bend them.
- Find success through the failure of others and yourself.

'Don't ask for permission, ask for forgiveness.'

- Invest in the time to gain new skills and competencies.
- Seek opportunities to expand your sphere of influence.
- Be part of the solution and not the problem.
- Experiment, take smart risks and learn from your mistakes.
- Apply what you have learnt to your daily situation.
- Do not get bogged down with detail.
- Be innovative, proactive and dynamic.
- Respond differently to situations.
- Life is a game know how to play the game (the aim is to win).
- Hate the game, not the players.
- Don't care about what other people think or say about you.
- Don't live to please other people. Please yourself.
- Have a clear goal for the future.
- Maximise your contacts.
- Be in a state of preparedness.
- Use your initiative.
- Make the right choices/make the choices work for you.
- Be politically and financially astute.
- Think bold!

- Make bold decisions.
- Think long term.
- Have the big picture in mind.
- Pay attention to what you believe works best for you.
- If you don't go you will not grow.
- Record and document what you have done.

> # Be yourself.
> There is something that you can do better than any other. Listen to the inward voice and bravely obey that.
>
> (Unknown)

- Chart your own course.
- Be your own coach.
- Face trouble head on.
- Trust yourself first and not others.
- Never invest more than you are prepared to give.
- Size does matter.
- Scrutinize your approach to work and life.
- Change your work style/approach.
- Be prepared to try new things.
- Reflect on your practice.
- Transform your life/career.
- Get the panoramic view - focus on the big picture, rather than on the detail.
- Always look for strategies to change your life.
- Nobody can make you feel inferior, without your permission.
- Know how to enjoy yourself and have fun.
- Be true to you.

'Nobody can make you feel inferior, without your permission!'

Mirror Challenge 'Development Plan' Exercise:

Date:

Development Objectives	Action (What do I need to do to achieve my development objectives?)	Resources (What are the resources that will enable you to achieve your objectives?)	Success Criteria (What will be my success criteria?)	Target Date (for Review & Completion)

Comments:

Mirror Check:

You need to START!

Stop procrastinating

Take control

Act in faith

Refocus your thoughts

Trust your instincts

Mirror Check:

You need to:

- **Create it**
- **Say it**
- **Believe it**
- **Do it!**

Have a Mirror Moment!

Chapter Eight

Results – What a Result!

The third '**R**' in the MIRROR is Results. Ever watched a match and at the end all you can say is – what a result! Ever completed a task, especially something that took you a long, long time (I could name a few) and the relief at saying: Finally, it's done. Completed. Yes. What a result. I have done it. It's finished. We have had a breakthrough. Ever had to burn the candle at both ends and work throughout the wee hours of the night? The only thing that soothed your aching mind, body and soul was the acknowledgement or feedback of a job well done. Mission accomplished. That was a result. Ever taken a test and waited on the results. I love this quote – 'The x-ray is only half of the story. The results tell the other half.'

'Never tell anyone your plans, just show them the results instead.'

The result is success, the outcome, the effect, the end, the product, the solution, the achievement, the accomplishment, the answer as well as the conclusion. The result is what you have learnt. The result is the breakthrough. The result is 'winning' or 'quick wins'. Know anyone who likes losing? I don't think so. We play games to win. Some commentators believe that life is a competition and that the aim is to win at all costs. However, success without integrity means nothing. We want a positive result in the end. That's what this chapter is about – getting there in the end no matter what.

There is meaning and purpose in life. Have you succeeded in terms of your purpose and what you want to do? Life is a journey filled with small steps and a bigger purpose. What have been your outcomes, successes, achievements and/or accomplishments? They are yours. Claim them. No matter what the obstacles, storms, trials and tribulations – you made it – you got there in the end. No matter what people told you or said about you, you have risen above it. Another of my favourite quotes is, 'when people go low, you go high'. The result is achieving what you want on your terms and no one else's. It's about mastering the rules of the game, until you can beat your opponent at their own game. When one door got closed, you built one. You have a tried, tested and proven system of staying up, no matter what the odds.

I love this quote which states, that 'although some of us, might be in the gutter, we are still looking at the stars.' No matter what life throws at you, you are still standing and you are still here. You have not allowed fear to get a hold of you.

'Were you knocked out or not out?'

The 'knock backs' are just as important as the highs and have made you the person you are. You have acknowledged and learnt from your mistakes and made adjustments. You have come out stronger on the other side. You may have been wounded and hurt but you have gotten back up and ready to go again. You may have been knocked down, but now you are a knock out!

You have been through the fire and the rain, you have been broken into pieces, but you are tougher and smarter. You have come out as pure gold. You did it and you should be pleased as well as proud of your achievements. You have gone through a process and seen it through to the end. You are not just a starter but a finisher and everything in between. As I often got told by my parents: 'If you don't put in the work, what results are you expecting?' Your result is what you are expecting to achieve. What are the consequences of the change? What do you want to see, hear, feel, and do? You have to focus on what brings results. It's about changing your thinking and actions to get a different result. Results come in all shapes and sizes. It's about starting the impossible that becomes the possible.

'Achieve great things'

Keys to Success

How do you achieve the results that you want?

Know Thy Yourself

Don't be like some people who look in the mirror, move away and forget who they are. Get to know yourself and find out who you are. Make a choice about who you are and what you want to be. Just focus on what you do and you will get amazing results. Persistence and perseverance are in your DNA. Don't be a mirror of someone's opinion. Find the '**you**' in you. Be connected to and with yourself. Be honest, authentic and real with yourself. Most importantly, always believe in yourself, it is the first secret to success. I recently saw someone who had taken a year off work, to be 'themself'; to 'find themself'.

When asked what was the year off like? They responded: 'Amazing.' It had been a time of deep personal reflection, soul searching and self-discovery. Not having to deal with the hustle and bustle of everyday life, the box being too crowded, the human 'rat race', they had gotten off the human treadmill or 'dreadmill' and had learnt to slow down, appreciate life and loved ones a whole lot more.

Learn to be accepting of yourself and others – their warts and all. You cannot outrun the past. Your eyes are for looking forward. Your past is just that; your past. Leave it there and move on. Look after your self-worth as it provides you with the confidence to make the difference. Be thorough and passionate about what you do. Be centred in who you are. Love what you do. If you don't love or like what you are doing; why are you doing it? It becomes a mindless and pointless exercise. Have a re-think about your life and future and take action. You have to hold your own. It's not what other people say or do, it's what you say or do that counts. Know who you are and don't be frightened or afraid of who you are. It does not matter that you might be a small fish in a big pond. There is room for you. Why not start with being the big fish in the small pond. What's wrong with that? The biggest room is the room for improvement. You can make the difference.

'The biggest room is the room for improvement.'

Have an appointment with destiny. Allow time for creative thinking and use your imagination. Remember to get the glow, you have to eat the lightbulb. The greatest motivator is belief. Believe in yourself and you will be great. Getting the results you want is about making the most of your opportunities and thinking about yourself at the same time. I dare you to be better than you can be. Sometimes, it's the simple things in life that we need to adjust or change to get better results. You have been given authority over your life. Take it. Don't wait for the light to appear at the end of the tunnel, just slide down and turn it on yourself. Appreciate who you are. Do it your way. Be one step ahead. Autograph your work and document your achievements. Success is a dream turned into reality. Have that dogged determination to succeed and get the results you want. You have resilience and you keep bouncing back, no matter what. You are not just a survivor, but a victor. Getting results means not quitting but staying the course. Your past cannot be your future. Remember to: Get up! Show up! Look up! Don't give up!

'Be something bigger than yourself!'

Dream Again

Your expectations equal results. It's time for second and third chances. There's a new chapter in your life. Create your own dreams and follow them until they are a reality. You are full of greatness and destiny. You cannot vote on your purpose. Do what you have to do. Life can be an ideal, ordeal or a new deal – what is it to be? I have realised that it's indecision that harms us and not the decisions we make. Your future and results are determined by the thoughts you have, the decisions you make and the actions you take. Your future and results are not determined by others, but by you. I love the saying which states when people tell you, you are too big for your boots – just get bigger boots. Have you pushed past fear and failure to reach your dreams? That's inside the mind of a winner.

It's hard hanging on to dreams. Don't think you can't dream anymore or again? Are you scared to dream big? Dream again and dream big. My dreams are just beginning. Continue to have dreams and even bigger dreams. I have learnt that life stops the moment you stop dreaming. Let your dreams be bigger than your fears, your actions be louder than your words and your results be greater than your expectations. Be strong and hang onto your dreams. It does not take courage to quit. Have breakthrough ideas. One of my favourite questions is: 'Is it inspiration or desperation' or in terms of eating food 'is it moderation and not desperation?' It's not where the inspiration comes from, it's where it leads to that matters. Explore many interests and pursue them. Give yourself the freedom to try new things, you will be surprised at the results. Challenge yourself. Draw back from the apprehensions and impossibilities. Find out what's important to you and what works best for you. Find the power in you and believe in yourself.

Your dreams need vision and your vision needs dreams. Believe in the dreams you've wanted to come true and give them every chance to. It may take years, but keep on working on it. I am reminded that Rome was not built in a day and it was not done overnight. But dreams do come true. Push past your fears and failures to reach your dreams. The result is all in the detail. You are the architect and blueprint of your life. It's about making your own rules and following them. Taking your own advice. You have to wake up each day and renew your commitments to yourself. Last year, my personal mantra was: 'It's time to jump without the parachute and forget about the distance.' Forget the fears or even the tears. All I know is, I am landing safely. Learn the art of negotiation. Remember the saying: 'In life you don't get what you deserve, you get what you negotiate.' Be a productive person. They always say if you want something done, ask a busy person.

Remember: Life's circumstances are not always what you wished, hoped or dreamt it might be. At times, you may be led in different directions that you never imagined or designed, but go with the flow. Go in the direction that the path is taking you.

'Dream big! Dream large! Spread out! Reach for it!' Dream Generational!

Life is not a sprint finish

I am in awe and truly inspired by the legend Usain Bolt, but I realise that life is not a sprint finish but a marathon. To get the results you want, many of us need to gain experiences or be on a journey. Success cannot be microwaved. There is a process that we need to go through, but many of us, do not want to go through it. We want quick fixes and we want everything now. It is said that the waiting is the hardest part. I remember the television advertisement, which said: 'Feed me now.' We want our problems solved yesterday. We live in a digital age, world and culture, where people are perpetually impatient and they want things now, in an instant. I realise that with technology, you either innovate or you die. Life is crazy, it's fast and 24/7, so things are now seen as too slow, too long and too late.

'There are no quick fixes in life!'

Let's be real and honest – I'll admit, I have no patience waiting around for things to happen anymore. They seem like eternity. I even get impatient waiting for the microwave to heat something up, the computer to load up or to access the internet. Many things are instant – instant drink, instant coffee, instant pot, faster broadband speeds, same day delivery, fast food, meals in minutes (or should it be seconds) to name a few. There is even a demand for instant results. We have a microwave mentality. I am getting better, I am learning to be patient, to take a step back and give myself a break to get even better results. Depending on your situation, you may not experience success or the result you want overnight. It's a gradual process, but there is success in the moment. Cherish those moments as they add up. Remember, the results will be yours. When the world expects you to follow the rules, write your own.

'When the world expects you to follow the rules, write your own!'

We keep on putting plasters on big wounds, thinking that we can fix everything. We can't solve problems like that and expect to get a positive result. We need to look at solving life's challenges differently. I am not fond of items of clothing that states: 'One size fits all.' Who came up with that sizing/idea? It's not practical and it does not fit. No one said it would be easy. It's not a sprint. It's progression that will see you through, that will get you the results that you want. Trust and enjoy the process and be dedicated to your craft. There is beauty in grafting, to get the results you want. For you to really move on, you have to get things in order. Disorder does not get you anywhere. Be optimistic rather than resigned, submissive, fatalistic and pessimistic. Your optimism will fuel motivation, impetus, enthusiasm, stamina and creativity. When you put out good energy you get good energy back. I love the quote which states: 'Less drama and more karma.' Practice makes permanent. Find time to do the things that you want to do. It's about working smarter, not harder. Did you know that hard work is overrated?

'Delivering results is your goal!'

Mirror Challenge Results Exercise:

Write down 101 crazy dreams!

**Why not Think big. Dig deep. Stretch yourself.
Challenge yourself!**

Author's Reflection

In terms of results - always give 100%:

12% on Mondays
23% on Tuesdays
40% on Wednesdays
20% on Thursdays
5% on Fridays!

Mirror Challenge Results Exercise:

Following Your own Advice

What's the one piece of advice you have always followed and why?

How did you find doing this exercise?

Mirror Challenge Results Exercise:

What is the one thing that you wanted to achieve?

If you achieved it – How did you do it? Let's re-visit achieving your goal.

How did you find doing this exercise?

Mirror Challenge Results Exercise:

Challenge Yourself!

What have you gained/learnt as a result of a challenge?

How did you find doing this exercise?

Mirror Check:

You need to:

- **Want it**
- **Do it**
- **Prove it**
- **Achieve it!**

'From amazing to incredible!'

Make Life Count – That's Life.

What would you say to the person looking in the mirror now? This is what I would say: 'Be positive and have a spectacular view of the future.' I would also say: 'You only get one life, one shot and I realise that there is no point in wasting it.' Your life is what you value. There is no one better to be than yourself. Make your one day – today. Embrace where you are. Have a fresh and unique take on life. Don't postpone your life. For me, my life has moved on. I have new chapters to write and new stories to tell. I am bringing stories to life and adding life to stories. Life matters. The purpose of life is to serve and show compassion. Embrace the life you have and make the most of what you have got. It is said that, you never meet an interesting person who has not suffered in some way or the other. Your strength comes from within. Renew your body, mind and soul.

Life is worth exploring and living to the fullest. Life is great at this moment. Make your focus be possibilities. If you are willing to take the opportunities

---

given and to utilise the abilities you have, you will constantly fill your life with special moments and unforgettable memories. I'd rather have memories than nothing at all. Feel confident with the person looking back at you. Tell yourself, you have got what it takes to succeed. Give yourself space to think and the courage to act. Recommit yourself to a life that you are meant to live. Add life to your days rather than days to your life.

Take part in the beauty of life. Have and live an enjoyable life. Most things in life are not perfect. Stop trying to obtain the unobtainable. On social media, everybody is a critic. Get off social media. Give yourself a break, an amnesty. Most of the images you see are 'touched up' and 'brushed up.' It's not a real body transformation. Someone's face is put on someone else's body. You don't need a body double.

'I am a HOPE dealer - Helping Other People Excel'

Women in particularly have been subjected to unrealistic beauty standards for many years and with the growth of social media, this has intensified. Is it all about getting 'likes' and the approval of the cyber community? Be real and live life to the fullest. Be an active participant or life will pass you by. Are you the person who has everything except life? We might be at our rope's end, but we are not at our hope's end. It's not a journey of 'nope', but a journey of 'hope'. I am a hope dealer. 'I believe in **H**elping **O**ther **P**eople **E**xcel' (**H.O.P.E**). Hope is power. Hope is the opposite of fear. We all need hope. Let's have some lessons of hope. Life can be tough but hope lifts and guides us through the challenges of life. Give those around you and beyond hope. I believe in hope over experience.

As long as you are on this earth, you cannot divorce yourself from life. We need to keep on living. Part of living is learning. We need to grow or else we will die! We need to continue to learn and improve ourselves. With progress, we go through a process! Stop putting barriers up and start breaking them down. You have had the blinkers on too long. Stop pulling down the shutters all around you! Life is a cycle, it's full of circles. Have you heard the song – 'The circle of life?' Whatever you give out, it will come back to you. Help those who are less fortunate than you.

'Did the unthinkable and accomplished the impossible!'

Work towards inner peace, so that you are able to give it to the world. I do not consider myself a workaholic, but rather a work enthusiast who loves what I do and has a real passion and flair for it. I think it worthy and a privilege that I am able to live out my passion as a teacher, educator and trainer. I will never be a perfectionist. It's not in my vocabulary, it's too time-consuming and it does not happen. I operate in a spirit of excellence. For me, excellence is the exceptional drive to exceed my expectations. Take a mirror with you each day and look at who is holding it or who is holding you back. Re-train yourself to look in the mirror. Embrace the mirror. It's time to press the re-set button. Re-set your priorities and focus, re-set your life and re-invest in your knowledge. Re-line the silver lining. Take special and personal ownership and responsibility for yourself. Work hard, but play even harder. The one thing of radiance in your life is just around the corner. Life is a precious gift in which anything is possible. Make history, re-write your destiny. To get the full results, get the full picture. Your future is indeed brighter and greater. Life is short, find your happiness. Make life count. Live a life that is worthwhile, purposeful and meaningful. What a result!

'Add life to your days rather than days to your life!'

Mirror Check:

There is no better time than right now to be happy

Happiness is a journey, not a destination

Work like you don't need the money

Love like you've never been hurt

Dance like no-one's watching

Sing like no-one's listening

Live like it's Heaven on Earth

Live simply, Give generously, Care deeply, Speak kindly.

Author's Reflection

Never regret a day in your life:

Good days give you happiness;

Bad days give you experience;

Worst days give you lessons

and best days give you memories.

Mirror Check:

Today I am

Yesterday I was

Tomorrow I will

Have a Mirror Moment!

Are you prepared to be challenged?

Take The MIRROR Challenge and see the results.

Make Amazing Happen!

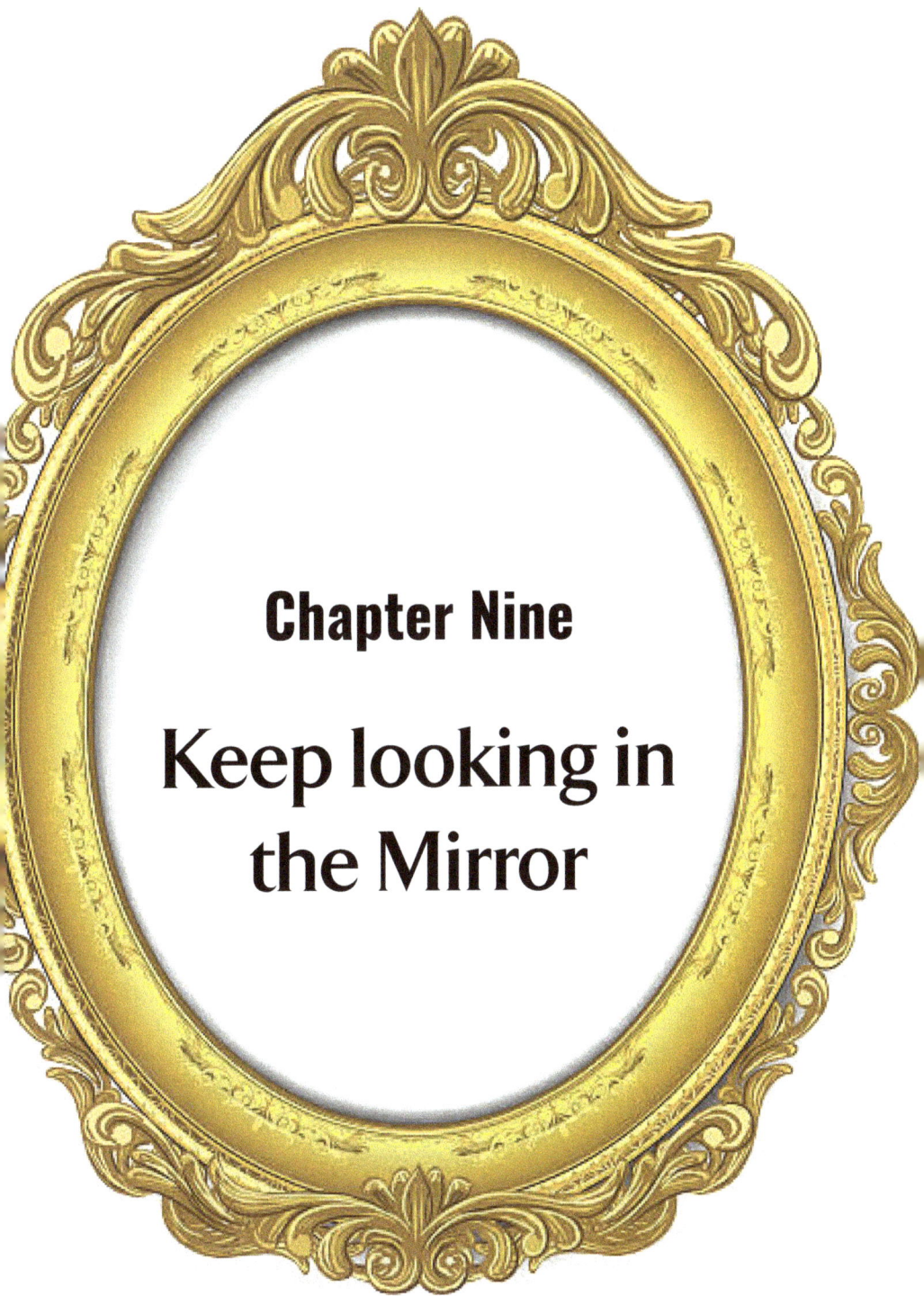

Chapter Nine

Keep looking in the Mirror

Great MIRROR Sayings

WHEN YOU LOOK IN THE MIRROR AND SEE NO CHANGE, AND STILL KEEP FAITH, KNOWING THAT IN TIME YOU WILL GET THERE IF YOU STAY FOCUSED AND ON TRACK, THAT'S THE DIFFERENCE BETWEEN THOSE WHO SUCCEED AND THOSE WHO FAIL.

"If you're searching for that one person that will change your life, take a look in the mirror."

Don't take mirrors seriously. Your true reflection is in your heart.

many people would be scared if they saw in the mirror, not their faces ... but their character .

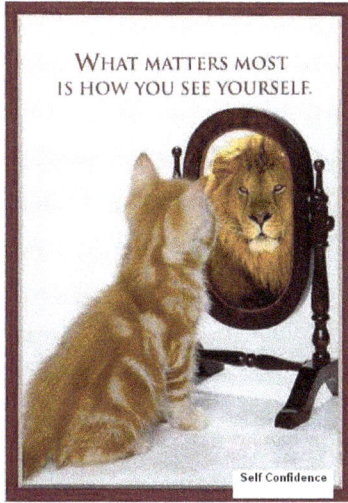

WHAT MATTERS MOST IS HOW YOU SEE YOURSELF.

Self Confidence

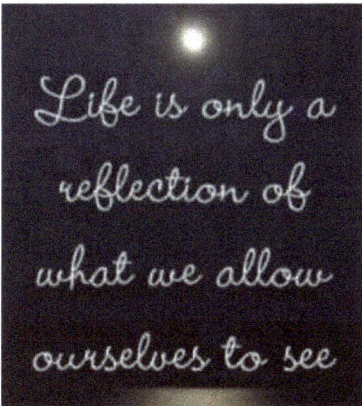

Life is only a reflection of what we allow ourselves to see

LOOK IN THE MIRROR... THAT'S YOUR COMPETITION.

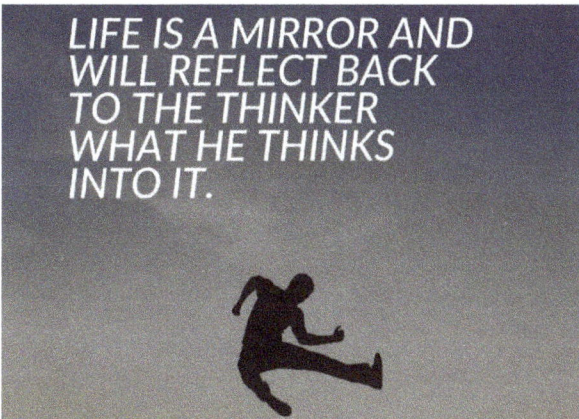

LIFE IS A MIRROR AND WILL REFLECT BACK TO THE THINKER WHAT HE THINKS INTO IT.

Chapter Ten

Training Programmes

The MIRROR Challenge™ – One and Two Day Workshop

Welcome to a fascinating and empowering session all about you.

Overview

The MIRROR Challenge™ is more than just a programme about improving your skills. It is a self-development, leadership and management tool which provides a structure for individuals, teams and groups to think, plan, do, review and take *real* action regarding their futures.

Petal reveals to businesses, professionals, managers, staff and individuals their innate ability to create new directions, opportunities and possibilities. It is an in-depth and hands-on programme, where individuals challenge their mind-set and thinking and gain mastery over their abilities and current situations and become their own agents for change.

An engaging programme, with its eye-opening concepts, demonstrations and exercises in managing change that gives individuals and teams the confidence and strategies, needed to become brilliantly successful in business, careers and life. This exciting programme gives you a fantastic opportunity to really challenge yourself.

Course Outline

Topics covered include:

- **The MIRROR Challenge™** is a self-development and management tool which provides a structure for individuals to think, plan and take action for the future. Remember: Think, Ink, Plan, Do and Review.

- Individuals are provided with an opportunity to prepare and create new directions, opportunities and possibilities.

- It aims to assist individuals in making informed choices, decisions and embrace change.

- Taking action to develop themselves and their careers, proactively.

- **The MIRROR Challenge™** provides practical advice on moving on and getting ahead in your career and life in general.

The more you look in the mirror, the more you will find out about yourself.

So, here's to looking in the Mirror, taking action and making those changes.

Tools and exercises will be provided so that you can practice the techniques and strategies covered in the workshop. These will also help you to think about strategies for managing change and moving on.

Give Yourself The Mirror Challenge.

The course is also offered in-house to companies and organisations. Group rates are also available. One-to-one coaching is available to help you apply what you have learnt at the workshop. Develop a clear understanding of your position, purpose and potential in life.

'The power of The MIRROR Challenge lies in its simplicity'

PLM Development Services
London SW16 4UW
Tel: 020 8764 1009
Email: info@themirrorchallenge.com
www.themirrorchallenge.com

The MIRROR Challenge for Business™ One Day Workshop

Welcome to a fascinating and empowering session all about you and your business.

Overview

This is an essential workshop for start-ups, established and growing businesses including:

- Freelancers

- Microbusinesses

- SME's

The workshop explores aspects of **The Mirror Challenge for Business™** programme developed by PLM Development Services.

Course Outline

Topics covered include:

- **The MIRROR Challenge** is a business development and management tool which provides a structure for individuals to think, plan and take action for the future. Remember: Think, Ink, Plan, Do and Review.

- It provides simple tools to enable you to focus on the most important asset of the business...YOU.

- Delegates and explore how to identify and leverage their personal and business assets.

● Provides an opportunity for delegates to think and plan for the development of a sustainable business.

● Enables participants to explore where they are now in their business and life in general.

The more you look in the mirror, the more you will find out about yourself and your business.

So, here's to looking in the Mirror, taking action and making your business work for you.

Tools and exercises will be provided so that you can practice the techniques and strategies covered in the workshop. These will also help you to think about strategies for managing and sustaining your business.

Give Your Business The Mirror Challenge

The course is also offered in-house to companies and organisations. Group rates are also available. One-to-one coaching is available to help you apply what you have learnt at the workshop. Develop a clear understanding of your position, purpose and potential in business.

'The power of The MIRROR Challenge lies in its simplicity'

PLM Development Services
London SW16 4UW
Tel: 020 8764 1009
Email: info@themirrorchallenge.com
www.themirrorchallenge.com

The MIRROR Challenge for Managers™

Who Is It For?

This is an essential workshop on self-management and being an effective manager. It provides the manager with a fantastic opportunity to be 'real' about themselves, examine, challenge, make changes and take action in terms of their management skills, styles and strategies. The workshop encourages the manager to do so in a way that helps them to grow as an individual as well as to further enhance their performance and results.

The workshop will explore aspects of the Mirror Challenge for Managers™ programme developed by PLM Development Services. It will identify best management practices as well as examine and discuss the skills, strengths, abilities, knowledge and practicalities of being an effective manager. It provides practising managers of all levels and stages of management, with the foundation for management development and success.

Workshop Outline:

- It makes sense, every once in a while to step back from the fast and changing pace of life and work and to ask yourself - Who am I? Where am I? What am I doing? How am I doing? Where am I going and where do I need to make changes in terms of being a manager? The key to life is management. How are you managing in terms of work and life?

- It is a self-development, leadership and management tool which provides a structure for individuals to think, plan and take action for the future. Remember: Think, Ink, Plan, Do and Review in terms of your management development.

- The Mirror Challenge for Managers™ workshop will provide simple tools to enable you to focus on the most important asset of management ...**YOU**!

- Managers are provided with an opportunity to prepare and create new directions, opportunities and possibilities.

- It aims to assist individuals in making informed choices, decisions and embrace change.

- Taking action to develop themselves and their management careers, proactively.

- The MIRROR Challenge for Managers™ provides practical advice on moving on and getting ahead in your career and life in general.

The more you look in the mirror, the more you will find out about yourself.

So, here's to looking in the Mirror, taking action, making those changes and taking those opportunities!

Give Yourself The Mirror Challenge!

The course is also offered in-house to companies and organisations. Group rates are also available. One-to-one coaching is available to help you apply what you have learnt on the workshop. Develop a clear understanding of your position, purpose and potential in business.

'The power of The MIRROR Challenge lies in its simplicity'

PLM Development Services
London SW16 4UW
Tel: 020 8764 1009
Email: info@themirrorchallenge.com
www.themirrorchallenge.com

The MIRROR Challenge for Children and Young Adults™

Who Is It For?

This is an innovative and a unique personal development workshop for Children and Young Adults. The essential aim of the workshop is finding out about **you**, using the Mirror Challenge for Children and Young Adults™ programme developed by PLM Development Services. We need to keep on learning about ourselves and others. Participants need to question themselves. It makes sense, every once in a while to step back from day to day activities and ask yourself – Who I am? What am I doing? Where am I? Where am I going? How am I doing? Where do I need to make changes? We also need to challenge young minds, break down stereotypes and challenge cultural mindsets. The programme is about shaping leaders for tomorrow. Participants need to continue to enhance their self-presentation and communication skills as individuals.

Aims:

There are a number of challenges and changes facing children and young people today. The programme aims to help Children and Young Adults to build and enhance their self-esteem and self-confidence. The workshop aims at improving an individual's motivation and attitudes towards education and for them to increase their learning independently. For participants, to develop a positive attitude towards the pursuance of goals and a healthy desire towards achieving success in all areas of their live. For Children and Young Adults to be ambitious in the right way as well as to see the importance of educational and personal achievement.

This programme provides an opportunity for individuals to think and plan for the future in a safe environment. Participants will be provided with an opportunity to plan and prepare for new directions and possibilities. It also aims to assist them in making informed choices and decisions and to take actions to proactively develop themselves.

The programme works with individuals and teams to identify and set achievable personal goals and steps they need to take to achieve them. It aims to assist Children and Young Adults in accepting self-responsibility for their behaviours and actions.

The key messages of the Mirror Challenge for Children and Young Adults™ include the following:

- Be the **best** in whatever you want to be or do.
- Any child or young adult can be whatever they want to be in life, as long as they want or are determined to succeed.
- Competition is healthy and learning should be fun.
- Self-discipline and focus have to be inculcated from an early age.
- It's better choices and decisions in life that are important and not the latest gadget or technology that will make the difference.
- Life is a journey and not a sprint and there are many milestones along the journey to be achieved.
- Work smarter, not harder.

The more you look in the mirror, the more you will find out about yourself.

So, here's to looking in the Mirror, taking action and making those changes.

'The power of The MIRROR Challenge lies in its simplicity'

PLM Development Services
London SW16 4UW
Tel: 020 8764 1009
Email: info@themirrorchallenge.com
www.themirrorchallenge.com

'Your Next Best Move'–Training and Coaching Programme

Aims:

The programme is specifically designed to support managers and staff who are exiting their organisation's services. It is geared at helping participants leave the organisation in a positive, pro-active and structured way. Leaving the organisation offers wonderful opportunities, but is also a major change and/or upheaval for many individuals. The aim is to equip individuals with the skills and techniques to fit emerging job and or business opportunities. The programme provides a safe environment in which participants will be able to explore how they feel, to plan for their futures and the changes that are to come. It provides the opportunity to examine life planning issues and strategies.

Topics covered include:

- **'Managing Change'** - I Day Course
- **Job Application Skills** - I Day Course
- **CV Writing Skills** - I Day Course
- **Interviewee Skills** – I Day Course
- **Self-Marketing/Presentation Skills** – I Day Course

Objectives:

- Coming to terms with your situation - Taking staff, groups and individuals through the change process.
- Change – what needs to change?
- Self-Auditing - taking stock - looking at and within yourself.
- Exploring transferable skills, abilities and competences for future roles/functions.

- Examining career alternatives and options such as Self Employment/ Being an Entrepreneur - Business Ideas and development as an option.
- Exploring the possibilities and opportunities that change offers/ provides.
- Covering CV Writing, Job search and strategies and Interviewing skills and techniques.
- Action planning for the future - working through personal action plans – to enhance future employment/career/business prospects.
- Lessening the anxiety people are experiencing, taking control, building self-esteem and confidence and taking care of their health and overall wellbeing.
- Personal well-being will be a constant theme that underpins all discussions, activities and exercises.

In-House Training

The programme can be presented exclusively for your organisation on an in-house basis, tailored to meet your specific needs. Group rates are also available. One-to-one coaching is available to help you apply what you have learnt on the workshop. You can:

- Have the programme designed for your specific needs
- Choose your preferred date and location
- Save on staff travel, time and accommodation costs

Maximise the impact of the training by putting an entire team through the same programme.

PLM Development Services
London SW16 4UW
Tel: 020 8764 1009
Email: plmtraining@aol.com
www.petalmiller.com

Looking for effective business development training for your managers and staff then talk to PLM Development Services

PLM Development Services is a learning, training and development consultancy that offers keynotes, workshops, seminars and training services designed to bring life to the workplace. We have a passion for motivating, inspiring and developing people to personal and professional fulfilment.

Through presentations with real-life application, PLM Development Services helps managers to become successful leaders and effective communicators and companies truly serve their customers.

We are widely known for our refreshing, thought provoking and informative delivery. You will appreciate our innovative and participatory techniques that produce immediate gains in your personal and professional productivity and learning.

Many organisations find that it suits their needs to incorporate a PLM Development event into their own training programmes. We can also design specific training courses to meet your business and individual needs. Topics available include:

- **Career and Personal Development**
- **Communication, Personal Impact and Effectiveness Skills**
- **Customer Services**
- **Health, Wellbeing, Care and Community Services**
- **Equality, Diversity and Inclusion Programmes**
- **Executive Coaching**
- **Supervisory and People Management**

- **Management Training and Development**
- **Leadership Development and Training**
- **Outplacement Support for staff – CV Writing, Interview and Presentation Skills**
- **The MIRROR Challenge ™**
- **Team Building and Development**
- **Training for Trainers**
- **Recruitment and Selection**

For Further information, call Petal L. Miller
PLM Development Services
London SW16 4UW
Tel: 020 8764 1009
Email: plmtraining@aol.com
www.petalmiller.com

Make an impact on your organisation through Learning, Training and Development

Don't Take Our Word for It . . .

Samples of Participants' Feedback

'The MIRROR Challenge workshop was part of a Human Resources (HR) Ambitions one day event. The whole day was well thought through and I attended the MIRROR challenge in the afternoon session.

I was intrigued by the MIRROR challenge as I was not familiar with this development tool. My initial assumption was that I would be holding up a metaphorical "mirror" to myself to determine what the reflection of my career was so that I could commence a strategy to develop my vocational aspirations. My assumption was far too vague. The key action for the MIRROR Challenge was "I dare you to.......!" Doing nothing was not an option in the session or in the examination of your aspirations.

The MIRROR challenge offered us a simple and effective personal development tool to focus our self-conversations about our own respective futures. The session broke down the MIRROR acronym to explain M = mirror, I = impact, R = reflect, R = respond O = opportunities, R = Result. Petal went through the interpretation of each, in order to fix this acronym in our psyche so we can call on it as and when we needed it; whether for ourselves or to use with others. So the MIRROR Challenge helped us to self-reflect and galvanised us into action.

Petal Miller was the course facilitator and she took us through an action packed session that was simply fun. Petal succeeded in involving the whole group without the session feeling laboured or uncomfortable. She commenced by asking us to work in pairs to challenge ourselves to "dare to" do or achieve something that we will promise to carry out. Delegates revealed their career aspirations and received sound advice from others in the group. She made the group laugh and she gave space to delegates who were making (or thinking of) a life changing decision.

Using PowerPoint to explain the theory and the provision of handouts and actively keeping us busy, she ensured that the message surrounding this tool was understood by all. The session was very interesting and Petal delivered a "feel good" element in her session as she was so upbeat, personable and entertaining. She emphasised that the MIRROR challenge was a challenge within yourself and you could not hold anyone else responsible for failing to apply the tool to yourself and hold back your potential. A large chunk of the session was taken up by the delegates so they had an opportunity to share their careers and aspirations, blocks and potential opportunities in safety. Petal completed the session leaving a genuine feeling of determination to move forward with our futures.

What I learnt at this session was that I had a simple, logical and flexible toolkit to help me frame my ideas for making decisions about my future and the handouts would be used for referral to remind me of the detail of the course. I was leaving my role as I did not believe I could progress in that organisation. I have used Petal's handouts and themes to frame my decision making process.

I would certainly recommend this session to others who find themselves at the same crossroad in their career. I hope that Petal continues to develop and adapt the MIRROR Challenge for schools, further education, coping with change and other significant key decision making and that coupled with her energetic and engaging presentation skills she will continue to inspire her audience'.

A. S. - November 2008

'Petal is one of the most gifted, talented and inspirational facilitators I have had the pleasure to work with. Petal has incredible knowledge and experience in a range of subject matters and is able to translate her knowledge and share this with delegates. I had the pleasure of hiring Petal on a number of occasions in the past. She always delivers high quality workshops which were "outstanding" not only for the delegates concerned in terms of achieving their learning outcomes but delivery against organisational outcomes. In addition, Petal is a world class coach, innovative in her approach and is always consistent and reliable. Petal has extensive expertise in human resources, learning and organisational development and always puts the customer at the heart of everything she does. I would have no hesitation in recommending Petal's work to any organisation. They will not be disappointed.'

A. M. - August 2011
Head of Organisational Development, Education and Leadership

'The session captured my attention from start to finish. Honestly, I cannot fault it. The material, the interaction with others was second to none. I have attended several placement seminars through my past employment and the Mirror Challenge; in its simplicity but very challenging, definitely encourages and brings to the forefront what and how we are to take stock of our lives and futures. It has enabled me to open my mind's eyes going forward and to things that are dormant in my life. I suppose I can relate this in a way to when employers conduct appraisals, which requires you to set goals and objectives (I have always struggled with appraisals but after attending the Mirror Challenge I recognise that there is MORE to Roslyn). I am inspired.'

R. J. - April 2009

'A great workshop with a nice balance. I found it to be really interactive, participative and it promoted discussion; which aided learning, gave food for thought, and was interesting and informative. A very useful day that was good in content.

Petal has a unique style to keep everyone interested and made it a very worthwhile session with practical guidance and left me enlightened and motivated.'

L. W. - April 2009

'This course gets you thinking. It was motivating and showed ways of improving myself. I will try to achieve more things that are tangible and visible and that will help clients.'

L. D. - January 2010

'The workshops are interactive, informative and Petal's style of delivery will have you wondering at the end of the workshop where the time went.'

J. H. - January 2010

'It gave me the opportunity to reflect on myself, both in the work environment and personally. I now know how and what needs to change. I loved listening to Petal's Mirror Challenge presentations. It leaves you re-evaluating yourself and has you viewing situations with a different perspective.

D. C. - December 2018 – January 2019

'It made me want to better myself and think about what steps I needed to take in order to do so. Very positive and uplifting. Petal made me see myself in a different light and how to turn negative things into positives. Thank You!!!'

T. J. - December 2018 – January 2019

'Loved every session. Very interesting and uplifting. Made me fearless and that I could be what I wanted to be.'

S. R. - December 2018 – January 2019

The Mirror Challenge for Business

'I attended this training course at the Social Enterprise Coalition Conference and I was really challenged and motivated.

Firstly, I have never heard Business Planning explained in such a way, as apart from examining what my strengths, challenges, opportunities and trials were; it also caused me to think about my life with reference to what I was doing and examine how to succeed and what measurements needed to be in place. What do I see when I look in the mirror, or like the woman who was talking, am I of the opinion that they don't even make good mirrors anymore? I was really motivated and the Challenge made me even more determined to succeed.

Thank you Petal for an inspiring time!'

S. L. - October 2009

Mirror Challenge Skills Exercise

List of Skills

This is not an exhaustive list and you can add even more.

1. Accountability
2. Action Planning
3. Adapting
4. Administration
5. Advertising
6. Advisory
7. Advocacy
8. Analytical
9. Anger/Aggression Management
10. Appointment Booking
11. Appraisal
12. Assertiveness
13. Assessment
14. Attention to Detail
15. Auditing
16. Body Language
17. Budgeting
18. Business Planning
19. Care
20. Care Planning
21. Chairing of Meetings
22. Change Management
23. Charting
24. Checking
25. Coaching
26. Communication
27. Complaints Management
28. Conflict Management/Dispute Resolution

29. Controlling
30. Counselling
31. Creative
32. Crisis Management
33. Customer Service
34. Data/Information Gathering
35. Decision Making
36. Delegation
37. Designing
38. Digital
39. Discipline/Grievance
40. Dismissal Management
41. Documenting
42. Drawing
43. Empathy
44. Empowering
45. Enabling
46. Enquiry
47. Environmental Management
48. Equality and Diversity
49. Evaluation
50. Facilitation
51. Fact Finding
52. Feedback
53. Financial Management
54. First Aid
55. Flexibility
56. Forward Planning
57. Goal Setting
58. Health and Safety Knowledge

59. Health and Safety Management

60. Human Resource/People Management

61. Implementing Policies/Procedures

62. Induction

63. Influencing

64. Information, Communication & Technology (ICT)

65. Information Management

66. Innovative

67. Interpersonal (1-2-1)

68. Interpretation

69. Interviewing

70. Intrapersonal (1-2-Group)

71. Investigative

72. Language

73. Leadership

74. Learning

75. Liaise/Liaison

76. Listening

77. Literacy

78. Management

79. Manual Handling/Lifting/Moving

80. Marketing

81. Meetings/Chairing

82. Mentoring

83. Methodical

84. Minute Taking

85. Monitoring

86. Motivational

87. Multi-Skilled/Tasked

88. Negotiation

89. Networking
90. Non-Judgmental
91. Note Taking
92. Numeracy
93. Observation
94. On Own Initiative/Workload
95. Oral/Verbal
96. Organisational
97. Partnership Working
98. People Management
99. Performance Management
100. Planning
101. Positivity
102. Presentation
103. Prioritising Workload/Workload Management
104. Problem Solving
105. Project Management
106. Progression
107. Public Relations
108. Quality Control Management
109. Quality Improvement Management
110. Questioning
111. Record Keeping
112. Recording
113. Recruitment and Selection
114. Reflective Practice
115. Report Writing
116. Research
117. Resource Management
118. Review

Keys to Effective Writing

- Accuracy
- Always proofread your work or get others to proofread it for you
- Aims and objectives are clear
- Appropriate to the reader - tone and level

- Be personal, polite and friendly
- Check your work through
- Clarity
- Concise

- Diplomacy
- Factual
- Format – finding what you need
- Illustration/interesting

- Keep your sentences short and simple (***K.I.S.S***)
- Keep your layout clear
- Provide or give information

- Punctuation – use them!
- Put your work to one side and go back to it later if you get stuck or go 'blank'

- Purpose of the communication
- Remember your role as a writer
- Remember your '***Rules for Writing***' before you send it out

- Structured – Introduction, Middle and End
- Structured – BBC – **B**eginning, **B**ody and **C**onclusion

- Structure documents in a logical order – My Six Best Friends - Who, What, When, Where, Why and How
- Summary and/or conclusion

- Think of your readers
- The Diamond Shape of Writing
- Use lists and bullets points
- Use only use words you and your reader understand – use everyday words

- Use 'Active' verbs instead of 'Passive' words
- Use your computer's spell and grammar check as appropriate. Keep a thesaurus/dictionary to hand and use it. Remember there is always 'google' or other search engines to help you
- Watch your '**GPS**' - **G**rammar, **P**unctuation and **S**pelling.

www.ingramcontent.com/pod-product-compliance
Lightning Source LLC
Chambersburg PA
CBHW041820090426
42811CB00009B/1048